What people are saying abo

"Make time for this worthy read! You will be blessed by Ginny's transparency and raw honesty. Much more than a book about her own road, though, Ginny roots *Singing in the Dark* in the grand narrative of Scripture, humbly and confidently turning our eyes toward our Redeemer. With a beautifully measured blend of testimony and Scripture, Ginny becomes more than a songwriter, singer, and theology student—she becomes a trusted companion on the journey."

Kelly Minter, Bible teacher, author
of *Finding God Faithful*

"With gentleness and vulnerability, Ginny Owens leads us into an exploration of the songs of the Bible. Few things speak to me from Scripture more than the expressions of deep longings, joy, and pain expressed by so many of the real human souls we meet there. I'm captivated by Ginny's ability to bring these passages to life by bridging to her own life. Who better than Ginny Owens to teach us all how to sing in the dark?"

Michael W. Smith, singer and songwriter

"While we might not know what it is like to live in the darkness of physical blindness like Ginny does, we all know what it is like to find ourselves living in other kinds of darkness—the darkness of disappointment, disillusionment, and difficulty. So what does it take to learn to sing the Lord's song in the dark? Ginny shows us. Blending her voice with the voices of people we meet in the Bible, Ginny helps us find our own voices to sing hope in the dark."

Nancy Guthrie, author of *God Does His Best Work with Empty*

"Ginny's music has been singing into my own personal darkness for over twenty years now. After my wife died of cancer, Ginny took words from Melissa's journal and turned them into the song 'If You Want Me To.' To this day, every time I hear it, I feel a very emotional and powerful connection. Ginny's heart flows through her music and her words, and I know *Singing in the Dark* will bless you."

Jeremy Camp, artist

"Ginny's masterful storytelling, personal transparency, and poetical exegesis help us revel in the hope we have, recover the hope we've lost, and lead image-bearers who feel completely bereft of hope toward the unconditional love and hope of Jesus Christ. This is more than a must-read; it's a literary keepsake!"

Lisa Harper, author, Bible teacher, speaker, women's ministry leader

"We often forget that God is not only fully present with us, but He sings over us with joy. Ginny's new book has deeply inspired me to sing a song back to Him. When we're hurting, lonely, or overwhelmed by His goodness, He wants to hear from us. You don't have to be a singer or a songwriter to put words to your story as an offering to God. Ginny writes in an honest, accessible way. Reading this book felt like a scenic walk with an old friend. Highly recommend it!"

Susie Larson, talk radio host, national speaker, author of *Prevail*

"In *Singing in the Dark* one of my favorite songwriters listens to some of the most important songs of the Bible and engages, resonates, and responds—and in the process encourages us to do the same. I've been waiting a long time for Ginny Owens to write a book, and *Singing in the Dark* goes beyond what I was hoping for."

Michael Card, Bible teacher, songwriter

Ginny Owens

SINGING
IN THE DARK

Finding Hope in the
Songs of Scripture

DAVID C COOK

transforming lives together

SINGING IN THE DARK
Published by David C Cook
4050 Lee Vance Drive
Colorado Springs, CO 80918 U.S.A.

Integrity Music Limited, a Division of David C Cook
Brighton, East Sussex BN1 2RE, England

The graphic circle C logo is a registered trademark of David C Cook.

Library of Congress Control Number 2020951248
ISBN 978-0-8307-8187-4
eISBN 978-0-8307-8188-1

The Team: Susan McPherson, Jeff Gerke, Judy Gillispie,
Kayla Fenstermaker, Jon Middel, Susan Murdock
Cover Design: Jon Middel
Cover Photo: Getty Images

Printed in the United States of America
First Edition 2021

1 2 3 4 5 6 7 8 9 10

022421

*To parents, Bible teachers, youth leaders, small group
leaders, pastors, and all who work to instill a love
of Scripture in the hearts and minds of those you
serve. Thank you for all you do. Never lose heart on
your mission, no matter how dark things seem.*

*To my fellow travelers on the journey to
love and understand Scripture more fully,
I pray that, in some small way, this book
moves you to hear its music more deeply.*

*To those who live amidst daily darkness, I pray
that as you read these pages, God will speak light
into your heart, in the ways only He can.*

Contents

Foreword

I met Ginny Owens more than twenty years ago when she and I were label mates on Rocketown Records. We became fast friends, probably because both of us were newbies to life on tour and, most of the time, the only two women on a bus full of men. An experience like this will bond you, as it becomes imperative that you have each other's back as women. I guess it's pretty ironic, then, that our most bonding moment as friends—hands down—has to be the time I accidentally caused Ginny to fall down a terribly steep flight of stairs!

She and I had just completed our life-on-tour bedtime routine in the women's restroom of whatever church or venue we had called home that day. We were extra chatty that night as we briskly headed to the bus that would carry us, while we slept, to the next place we'd call home for the day. And then it happened. I got about two steps in, down that monstrous flight of stairs, and Ginny started to tumble. Head over heels, down she went and there was nothing I could do to stop her! Terrified that I had caused serious injury to my friend, I raced down after her, grateful that I could hear her talking to me and see her moving all her limbs. One of the tour managers helped me get her onto the bus and started tending to her wounds as I sat next to her apologizing over and over:

"Ginny! I'm so sorry! I forgot you were *blind!*"

It's the honest truth. In fact, I forget that Ginny is blind a lot of the time. I can remember a few times even elbowing her in the side to say, "Ginny, *look!*" before I even realized what I was saying. Or when I'd drop her off in her hotel room on tour, I'd flip on the lights for her before I'd leave. She'd hear the click of the light switch and smile her cheeky grin and say, "Thanks!"

But this was no excuse—I should never have let this happen; I was her *wingman* for crying out loud! If she was Frodo, I was her Sam in those days, and she was counting on me. All I could think about was when you're given the very important task of guiding a blind person, not only should you stay aware of the fact that she is blind, but you most certainly need to give her a heads-up that you are about to head down a flight of stairs!

"It's okay. I love that you forget I'm blind," Ginny said. There she was, comforting me while having gravel tweezed out of her busted-up knees.

The way I look at it, Ginny's physical eyes may not work the way mine do, but I assure you, she *sees*. In fact, I think she's developed some "Spidey sense" over the years, almost a sixth sense when it comes to what's going on around her. Ginny has spent most of her life in physical darkness and has endured some very trying seasons that she's been open to sharing in this book. But it's clear to me that God intended all along for a spiritual sight to develop in Ginny's heart, one that would birth songs of surrender, hope, and freedom— and not just in her own life but in the lives of others.

I believe this is what God has in mind for all of us as we walk through darkness, brokenness, and difficult seasons. I believe He will even use the most trying hardships of our lives to heighten our senses to the nearness of His presence. In fact, I've learned that we can even begin to look at the "hurry up and wait" and the "things didn't go as planned" seasons of our lives as an invitation. One that encourages us to set the eyes of our hearts on Jesus, especially when we cannot see or fathom in the natural how He's going to come through for us. With our gaze lifted to Him, we're able to see Him for who He truly is. And like my friend Matt Redman often says as he leads worship, when we *see*, we *sing*. When we truly encounter God with the eyes of our hearts—especially in the dark—we cannot help but sing!

It makes me think of Paul and Silas, in Acts 16, when they shook the walls of their prison cell with praise. The passage clearly states that they began to worship around midnight. I've heard it said that maybe their praise arose *because* it was pitch dark in their prison cell. Think about it: they couldn't see the iron bars or the shackles that bound them; all they could *see* was a God of hope and freedom, and they surrendered to His song.

I realize that while this sounds inspiring, it might also sound too good to be true—to think that you and I could learn to *sing* through trials, hardships, and the darkness this world throws at us at every turn. I'll tell you this: Ginny is lovingly transparent in this book as she shares what I believe is the key to truly learning to sing in the dark. It's not about our developing an inner strength to keep us going or a hustle that has us trudging and gritting our teeth through the dark. It's about trusting God, even surrendering to His lead, as He's the only One we can truly trust to guide us in every season. In fact, I believe this is why God responds and even acts on our behalf when we surrender. He too trusts only Himself—not us or anyone else—to faithfully lead us.

His Word tells us in 2 Chronicles 16:9, "The eyes of the LORD range throughout the earth to strengthen those whose hearts are fully committed to him" (NIV). I like to imagine Him on the edge of His seat, looking for those who might lock eyes with Him—especially in the darkest seasons of our soul—that we might begin to sing of who He is, even coming to know Him as the God who *sees* and *sings* too (Zeph. 3:17).

You know what's really beautiful? As you learn to sing in every season, your song will begin to bellow out beyond just a melody coming from your mouth. Your *life* will begin to sing! Beloved, this is why God wants to teach you to sing in the dark: that the songs that form in you might begin to pour out *from* you, bringing joy, freedom, and hope everywhere you go.

Christy Nockels

2020

Before You Begin

I am at heart a painter. Give me a smooth canvas and a palette with oils, and I lose myself in composition and color. Rural landscapes are my thing, especially ones that draw the viewer down a winding country road or along fields of wheat that disappear into a long, endless blue. To paint is to breathe. It is my way of expressing how the world moves me and touches my heart.

I cannot hold brushes, though. Decades ago, I broke my neck in a diving accident and lost the use of my hands. But I did not lose my artistic bent, a talent I absorbed from my artist father. Although I cannot pick up a brush with my fingers, I am able to clench one between my teeth—I swirl oils across a canvas in a way that's different from most artists.

This has made me a better painter. It's made me think more. Spend more time reflecting. It has also driven ideas deeper into my heart, where, over time, they settle and simmer. They linger long there until they surface, bright, beautiful, and demanding to be painted. I love when that happens. It makes for *great* renderings.

The same is true for my friend Ginny Owens. She also paints, but with music and lyrics. Like me, she lost an important physical ability—her blind eyes cannot guide her fingers across the seven octaves on a piano. But I have a feeling her blindness helps her think and reflect more until the music surfaces from her soul and spills out onto the keys, demanding to be played. I bet she loves when that happens. Yes, Ginny sings and writes in a way that is different from most artists.

And it makes for *great* music. I should know. Over the years, the songs of Ginny Owens have provided the musical background to my life of loss. I listen to the smooth way she slides through her own powerful lyrics, and I sense, *Here's a woman who understands suffering.* And those hardships have helped her embrace a sweeter intimacy with the Savior. In this way, Ginny encourages me to sing through my own times of darkness, of walking through the valley when He asks us to.

I think you can see why Ginny's songs have meant so much to me. Most likely you will never break your neck or walk through the world blind. But to borrow the words of Jesus, "In this world you will have trouble" (John 16:33 NIV). You *will* experience loss. It's why I'm so glad you are holding in your hands Ginny's latest work, *Singing in the Dark.*

This book is the best of guides as our friend steps away from her piano and pours out her creativity on paper, describing how God led her through her own dark seasons of suffering. Ginny shares how God sang to her, soothing her troubled soul with His own music from Scripture. Here is a gifted communicator who will help you learn how to sing your way through the night and out into brighter days filled with sunlit hope.

So pour a cup of your favorite coffee, get comfortable, flip the page, and get to know a fresh side of Ginny Owens. Keep a pen handy, for like any disciplined artist, she will ask you to put your own creativity to work at the end of each chapter. Take her up on it. Be brave. It'll make you think and reflect more. Let your ideas go deep and linger long until they surface and spill out onto the page, expressing how the world moves *you*. How Jesus touches *your* heart. How God leads you in *your* nighttime of loss.

You'll love it when that happens. Great things like that *always* happen when you learn to sing in the dark.

Joni Eareckson Tada
Joni and Friends International Disability Center
2020

Introduction

I was a senior in college when I first witnessed music bringing light into darkness. I was student teaching, learning to overcome my shyness and lack of stature to manage choir and piano classes at a large, multi-ethnic public high school in Nashville, Tennessee. I hoped to wow the world (or at least my supervising teacher) with my choral conducting skills.

But when I wasn't in class, I didn't spend my time passionately practicing our pieces for the coming months. Instead, I wrote my own songs, many of them about my students. My mind was full of the stories they'd confided in me, and songwriting was how I sorted out what I'd say to them if I got the chance.

I never wanted them to know I was a songwriter, though. My melodic musings weren't nearly as brilliant as the masterfully crafted pieces by Rachmaninoff that I was teaching the madrigal singers or the deep, dark, history-laden spirituals that the concert choir was learning.

Everything changed in my last week of student teaching. A friend kindly dropped by the classroom to give me a ride home at the end of the day, and after I coerced some of my kids into singing for her, she asked which of my own songs I had played for them. They had not, of course, heard anything I'd written.

I felt mortified—both that my friend had opened this door and at the students' ensuing insistence that I play something. After some protest, I figured we could all go home if I just got it over with.

And so, with my fingers shakily settling onto the piano keys and my voice sounding small and shy, I sang:

> *Angry words are spoken*
> *And the pain cuts deeper than a knife …*
> *But all the angry words you've ever heard can melt away …*
> *All because of His love and what He did that day.*

How often I'd wanted to say those words to so many of those kids. I fought back tears as I sang.

But the kids didn't fight *their* tears—they flowed freely. They connected with the words and music I'd written about God's love for them—and mine.

Over the next several days, word spread through my classes that I wrote songs, which resulted in me playing more of them. The words born out of my own hope and pain—and my desire to pour hope into their lives—connected. This led to many more students confiding in me about their loneliness and deep pain—hard times at home, broken relationships, too many days of dimming the darkness with drugs. Those stories opened the way for me to share some of my own personal struggles and encourage them with the hope that grounded me.

And it all started with one shared song.

I'd loved music since I was a baby, singing along to everything from the albums of an obscure children's music artist named Marcy to every song my ears picked up from the car radio. After I boldly belted out the lyrics to the KC and the Sunshine Band hit "Shake Your Booty" in front of a group of family friends, my parents gently explained we would be taking a break from listening to pop radio. It was, in their words, "trash music." I was so sad. "Trash music" had delivered the most delightful sounds my three-year-old ears had yet heard!

During the years when listening to pop music was banned, I played the songs I learned at church and school on the old piano that lived in the back corner of our dining room. After the millionth round of "Twinkle, Twinkle, Little Star" and "Jesus Loves the Little Children," I started experimenting with my own melodies and lyrics.

One night after bath time when I was seven, I was inspired to compose my first full masterpiece:

> *Don't forget the water,*
> *Don't forget the soap,*
> *Don't forget the bathtub,*
> *Or you'll have to give up hope.*
> *Don't forget Christ Jesus,*
> *He who cleansed your soul,*
> *'Cause He's the only One*
> *Who can make you whole.*

I thought it was a brilliant imitation of the Amy Grant songs I'd been listening to. No one I played it for seemed to agree.

But as I sang about cleansing the body and soul, I was learning the feeling of a heavy heart. *Divorce* became a new word in my vocabulary when my parents explained, after a lengthy separation, that this was the next step. I knew they didn't love me any less, but there was a certain weight to everything now that they weren't together. At the same time, I was finding out how it felt to be bullied and excluded at school. Being the creative, thoughtful, shy type didn't help matters, but I also had a physical challenge that seemed to invite unkindness.

I had lost my eyesight when I was three because of optic atrophy and several degenerative eye conditions. I couldn't help wondering whether that was the reason for all the chaos in my life.

Having no answer, I turned to music for solace. When my dad took me on a father-daughter date to dinner and the Jackson, Mississippi, city auditorium to see a traveling Broadway production of *Annie*, I was instantly obsessed. My eight-year-old heart fell in love with every song that emerged from Annie's delightfully dramatic life. I imagined all we had in common and willed myself to have red hair, a massive mansion, and a great group of friends from the orphanage. As I belted out the songs along with the soundtrack, I believed with Annie that tomorrow would be better.

When I wasn't listening to *Annie*, I was lost in the tender, thoughtful ballads of Amy Grant's early albums. Her gentle, vulnerable voice perfectly collided with her heartfelt lyrics as she sang about being hidden away from the chaos in God's powerful, loving arms.

About the same time, our church bought me a hymnal in braille, a book roughly twelve inches thick. Picture the largest single-volume reference book you can imagine. I spent many hours flipping its pages and singing its contents, making up melodies for the lyrics of songs I didn't know. One of my favorites was that of another blind girl, who had, a century ago, proclaimed her hope in the darkness:

> *Perfect submission, all is at rest;*
> *I in my Savior am happy and blessed.*
> *Watching and waiting, looking above,*
> *Filled with His goodness, lost in His love.*
> *This is my story, this is my song,*
> *Praising my Savior all the day long.*
> *This is my story, this is my song,*
> *Praising my Savior, all the day long.*[1]

Though I was still too young to fully comprehend the ornate language, the depth of the message cut straight to my heart: I could praise, looking above, no matter what was going on around me.

My soul soaked in every lyric of these rich, eloquent hymns and songs of faith, but I also adored singing along with the hopeful and heartbroken artists on the radio when the ban was lifted. Some days I wondered why they seemed so melancholy, and some days I could completely relate. Music expressed feelings I could not yet articulate. And God regularly spoke to my heart through the songs on my lips.

As a singer-songwriter who has spent my adult life sharing my music with people through albums and at concerts, I have repeatedly witnessed the life-changing impact that songs have on the soul. I've heard stories of how lyrics have helped invite freedom from long-time struggles or moved listeners to accept their current circumstances with hope.

I've been blessed to help teens craft songs about living with cancer, and I've seen military veterans with PTSD find new hope by framing their difficult stories in melody and lyrics. I've watched children who have lost their parents gain strength through writing songs that express their pain, and I've taught the nuances of songwriting to college students ready to set the world on fire.

This book is called *Singing in the Dark* because it's something I have been learning to do since those early years of voicing joy and sadness along with Amy and Annie in my bedroom. And it's something I believe we can all do.

We all experience darkness. Perhaps the darkness has come in the form of a painful loss, a chronic or terminal illness, deep loneliness, addiction, or perpetual anxiety and sadness. Whether you resonate with one of these categories or not, because you're a human being, you know what it is to do battle with darkness.

There's the darkness that keeps us from clearly seeing the path ahead, the haze of uncertainty as we make our way through the world. And there's the darkness that keeps us from face-to-face encounters with God this side of heaven, calling us to rely on faith (1 Cor. 13:12). But in any darkness we face, I am certain we can learn to sing of hope. True, deep, unshakable hope that comes from knowing that God broke into our darkness, conquering it once and for all.

This book is about more than just warbling a song—it's about creating and practicing a *mind-set*, one that I am convinced is the only way to walk through this life with joy in every circumstance.

We all long for wholeness. For perfection. So we do our best to avoid the brokenness within and around us. We block it out, or we turn up the noise of our busy lives to distract ourselves. We pretend the darkness doesn't exist. We choose not to sing.

But what if we did? What if we sang songs of hope in our darkness? Of lament in our pain and brokenness but also of the coming wholeness? What if we sang of both our suffering and our coming glory? What if we sang of the eternal joy that will outlast and ultimately triumph over our sorrow? Wouldn't such songs give us the hope and joy to overcome the darkness now?

Ignoring the darkness doesn't make it light. Avoiding brokenness doesn't bring redemption. But singing in the dark can heal us and change us. When our songs are directed toward God, the giver of song and healing, they ultimately bring us hope and joy. It takes courage to sing in the dark, especially in the moments when our stories don't make sense to us. When confusion and doubt overwhelm us. But this courage, it seems to me, grows as we sing.

In songwriting, I always draw deeply from personal experiences of the joy and brokenness in my own story. And as a Christian, I can sing because I have confidence about how things will turn out. Because God came to earth in Christ—living a perfect life and carrying our guilt to His death, experiencing utter human hopelessness before rising from the grave and ascending to heaven—we can rest in His finished work. Our lives on this planet are merely the beginning of our never-ending story—of God's never-ending story. But how can that bring us hope in the here and now?

The great King David wrote beautiful songs in which he poured out the heaviness in his heart. In nearly every instance, as he sang of the God he knew, his songs of mourning became songs of joy. Leah—David's humble, unattractive, unnoticed great-grandmother—sang songs of unfulfilled longing as she ached for her husband's love. But finally her heart sang peace and praise when she recognized that God was the provider and protector whose love had surrounded her all along.

Centuries later, Paul the apostle, whose letters make up much of the New Testament, sang to his friends the Philippians from prison: "I have learned the secret of being content in any and every situation" (Phil. 4:12 NIV). What was Paul's secret? How did Leah praise God when life seemed overwhelmingly lonely and unfair? What did David know about living with a song always in his heart?

David, Leah, Paul, and many others experienced profound hope in the midst of their darkness. In the unfolding of their stories, we see that hope and peace came as they sang—that is, as they voiced joy and sadness, praise and repentance, laughter and lament—to God. When we follow suit, not only do we hear the truth of our own hearts, but God, who sings over us (Zeph. 3:17), hears our songs too. And He works through them to draw us closer to Himself.

Many people view the Bible as a virtually inaccessible ancient book, with a few stories and psalms here and there that might be useful for comfort and guidance. Perhaps you have thought of the Bible in this way. I've had moments of treating it as such. But as I've plumbed its depths over the years, I've learned that this could not be any further from the truth.

My prayer, as we open the Scriptures together, is that we will be moved by the living, breathing Word of God, whose contents are relevant for every moment of our lives. The Bible is also our hymnal—our ultimate worship album—teaching us perfectly how to sing in the darkness of our circumstances.

I'd like us to explore several biblical passages to discover how, since the beginning of time, God's people have been singing their way to eternity. Some of the songs are not literal songs but heart songs. In each chapter, we'll explore one of these songs and link it with the bigger picture of God's plan for the world. We'll see how God's people became hopeful by singing to Him, and how we can too. We'll also memorize portions of these songs together so the profound richness of their truths can sing to us all day long.

To encourage you further, I'll be telling my own story along the way, a personal testimony of the power of learning to sing in the dark. I'm also going to invite you to compose songs of your own—the prayers and cries of your heart.

If you've been singing your life's songs in the darkness of sadness, physical suffering, self-doubt, or isolation, or if you simply want to learn to sing hope, no matter your circumstances, I invite you to join me as I share my story and we study the songs of Scripture. Together, we'll embark on a journey that I pray and believe will help you experience the infinite hope and endless joy we've been promised in Christ.

Leah conceived, gave birth to a son, and named him Reuben, for she said, "The LORD has seen my affliction; surely my husband will love me now."

She conceived again, gave birth to a son, and said, "The LORD heard that I am neglected and has given me this son also." So she named him Simeon.

She conceived again, gave birth to a son, and said, "At last, my husband will become attached to me because I have borne three sons for him." Therefore he was named Levi.

And she conceived again, gave birth to a son, and said, "This time I will praise the LORD." Therefore she named him Judah. Then Leah stopped having children.

Genesis 29:32–35

Chapter 1

A Song of Undivided Praise

The Search for Satisfaction

I wish you could know my brother, John David (JD for short). Despite being a highfalutin Marine Corps captain, he is one of the most high-spirited, life-loving people you'll ever meet.

When we were kids, JD lived by the mantra "My life would be perfect if I just had this one thing."

It's an idea most of us embrace, even as adults; JD just expressed it more boldly and more frequently than others. When he got his driver's license, he inherited our mom's old Ford Taurus. After installing a more powerful stereo, which made the speakers rattle constantly, even at a low volume, he put on huge rims and tires. It was the perfect car for a moment. But by Christmas, he was over it. The rattling speakers were annoying and shorted out often, and his gargantuan rims had gone out of style.

Soon JD was begging our parents to let him buy an old used black truck he'd found at a car dealership. When I went home for a monthlong break from college, it was all he could talk about. After several weeks of begging and wheeling and dealing, he finally got his new old truck. And for an instant, all was well. But the decrepit truck had little life left, and the love affair soon ended when the truck died for good. JD had to return to driving the Taurus with the big tires and rattly speakers, longing for a better set of wheels.

Like my brother, I tend to obsess over getting the things I'm sure will make life everything it should be. I play the piano but have always wanted to master the guitar. So I'm the proud owner of three guitars and two ukuleles—acquiring each in the hope that it would be easier on my piano-playing fingers and catapult me into guitar-playing success. I've bought kitchen appliances I was sure would inspire me to cook like a professional chef and exercise gear that would motivate me to work out. I've had lonely seasons as a single woman when I've been convinced that having a husband would make everything better. And the list goes on.

What would bring you satisfaction? For all of us, there is some-thing—one thing at any given moment—that we think will make us happy. Maybe a glance in the mirror on a bad hair day and a new skin flaw motivate you to switch to fancy hair-care products and pricey anti-aging cream. Perhaps a look at your bank account makes you long for a better-paying job. Or after a day of chasing or carting around your kids, you fantasize about a month alone on a beach.

For most of us, the things we'd like to change go much deeper: A lonely marriage. A job that requires navigating difficult relation-ships. An unexpected and unwelcome diagnosis. A challenge that accompanies us everywhere. Whether the thing we'd like to change is a slight nuisance or a dead weight, we spend our days looking for hope. Most of us have in our minds one thing we think would make everything better—one thing that would satisfy us.

Many of us have grown up hearing that God alone is the One who brings peace and fulfills our every need. Yet we aren't convinced. We're pretty sure, in fact, that what we need from God is not God Himself but the things He can give us—if He just would.

So what do we do when satisfaction is just out of reach? How do we sing of hope and gratitude when God isn't giving us what we want?

I'd like to explore with you the story of Leah, the granddaughter-in-law of Abraham and one of the first matriarchs we encounter in the Bible. Leah found herself in a miserable situation over which she had no control. And after years of longing for the one thing she thought would change everything, she found the One who truly did.

As we open Leah's story together, I'll also share a bit of my own story and how I, like Leah, found real, tangible hope and the satisfaction I had been longing for. My prayer is that Leah's song and mine will guide you to sing your own song of true, deep, joyful satisfaction, no matter what circumstances you're facing.

The Power of Desires

The story of Leah reminds me that, from the beginning of time, people have been facing impossibly challenging circumstances and coming up with their own ways to cope. Leah's plight as an unattractive older sister and the further struggles she faced because of her dysfunctional family have long captivated me. In her story we see how misplaced desires destroyed her family's happiness and peace. But we also witness how Leah finally found hope, even when her world didn't change for the better.

Let's see how the stage is set for Leah's grief. The story opens in Genesis 29 with Jacob, grandson of Abraham and younger son of

Isaac, running for his life. Jacob had successfully tricked his aged, blind father into blessing him rather than his slightly older twin, Esau, and giving him the inheritance usually meant for the older son. Fearing his brother's reaction, Jacob escaped to the eastern land of Paddan-aram to find his uncle Laban.

Upon arrival, Jacob met Laban's beautiful daughter, Rachel, as she herded her father's sheep. Instantly smitten by her beauty, he eagerly offered to work for Laban for seven years in exchange for Rachel's hand in marriage. Jacob had yet to realize that he and his uncle were cut from the same cloth. Instead of promising him Rachel's hand in marriage, Laban merely said, "Better that I give her to you than to some other man" (v. 19). But Jacob took that as a yes.

When Jacob neared the end of his seven years of labor, he went to Laban and insisted on a wedding to Rachel. Laban put on a great wedding celebration but tricked Jacob by giving him his older daughter, Leah, instead. We're not told exactly how this took place without Jacob's notice. However, because a bride would have been veiled throughout the wedding festivities, wine would have been freely flowing, and Jacob and Leah would have headed to their "honeymoon suite" when it was dark out, we can see how it could happen.

The next morning, after Jacob awakened to find he was married not to Rachel but to her older sister, he confronted his uncle turned father-in-law. In the end, Jacob agreed to another seven years of work in exchange for marrying Rachel too. Note that all this happened in Jacob's first week of marriage to Leah.

The Bible is full of stories you could not make up. Marrying two sisters at the same time was explicitly prohibited by the Lord (Lev. 18:18), and there is no doubt why. But here the Scriptures offer us a candid look at a dreadful situation. We sense how dangerous and destructive life became when Laban and Jacob were driven solely by their desires for what they thought would make them happy.

Laban wanted success, so he did everything he could to keep Jacob's skill set and business mind on his team indefinitely, including tricking him into fourteen years of work.

Jacob would stop at nothing to start a family with beautiful Rachel.

Laban's and Jacob's dogged determination to get what they wanted no matter what had a lasting impact on their family, and the first person it wreaked havoc on was Leah, the unloved and unwanted wife and daughter helplessly trapped in the web of chaos they had created.

Being a woman in ancient times meant that you belonged to your father until you belonged to your husband and that you didn't have a say in who that husband would be. Leah's prospects for marriage were likely not good because, we are told, she was not pretty. Her "eyes were weak, but Rachel was beautiful in form and appearance" (Gen. 29:17 ESV).

In Leah's day, eyes were considered a key component of beauty. Leah's eyes might have been small or a "weak" color; whatever the case, since they are compared with Rachel's beauty, we know the story is commenting on her unattractiveness. And because she wasn't pretty, she wasn't marriage material. She didn't get a special wedding celebration of her own. Instead, her father sneakily married her to the man who loved her sister. Poor Leah was thrown into a situation of hopelessness and loneliness.

Once married, she was determined to win her husband's love and acceptance. She undoubtedly believed his love would bring her happiness and peace. And though this desire became her deepest longing and drove her every move, it was never fulfilled.

Longing to Belong

Though most of us living in the twenty-first-century Western world can't relate to Leah's exact situation, we know how it feels to face rejection and the deep pain and frustration of circumstances we cannot change. We probably also know what it is to dream of and long for one thing we're sure would make everything better.

My own journey has involved learning to live with things I can't change. I was born with weak eyes, though in the more literal sense. Just about the time I was learning my colors—apparently my favorite was purple—I underwent a cryotherapy treatment that obliterated what little sight I had. My parents say I stayed in bed for six weeks afterward; then I got up one day and went back outside to play as if nothing had ever happened.

As a young child, being blind never slowed me down. I rode my bike all over the neighborhood and competed with my friends on the block to be the highest tree-climber. Blindness became important only when I went to school.

It didn't take long for the other kids—and me—to realize that they could see and I could not. As the understanding dawned that my inability to see bothered them, I became more self-aware and very shy. And as they left me out of their games or waved their hands in front of my face, demanding to know how many fingers they were holding up, my fearlessness turned into sadness.

One Sunday morning, as all the other first graders laughed and colored together, our Sunday school teacher said, "Everyone who puts their eyes up here right now will get to make a very special craft today." The room grew silent as everyone obediently looked at her and received the promised opportunity to make the paper-plate angels—everyone but me. As I sat alone at a table, I wondered, *Does this make me a nobody? Do I count as a person, since I can't see?*

My parents were wonderfully intentional about making sure I understood how the world worked and what I'd need to do to fit into it. But as each new piece of the puzzle of awareness fell into place, I also understood with increasing clarity my "differentness" and the fact that acceptance by others was key for a "normal," fulfilled life. I realized sometime during elementary school that my circumstances would not change, and from then on, the desire to belong took center stage. It became that "one thing" I thought I had to have to be happy.

Leah's Songs

For Leah, the "one thing" she longed for—the thing she believed would quiet the chaos and bring peace—was to be loved by her husband. Yet the thing that actually brought her peace was the love of her God.

The most compelling part of Leah's story is not the difficult, dark place in which she found herself but how God moved in her circumstances—lifting her out of her darkness and giving her a key role in His greater story. Leah was consumed by her longing, but as she turned to God in her anguish, He showed her that He saw her and loved her perfectly and was the only answer to her deep desire.

A beautifully poignant key to understanding the story of Leah is her "songs," the declarations that she made at the birth of each of her first four children. These songs reveal how God worked in her heart, slowly changing her point of view.

Even in our most seemingly impossible situations, God always has the final word. "When the LORD saw that Leah was hated," the Bible says, "he opened her womb" (Gen. 29:31 ESV). Here we get to witness how God truly and deeply sees each person, whether that person *feels* unseen or actually *is* unseen by others. Leah responded to being seen by God by naming her first child Reuben, which in Hebrew means "Look! A son!" The name connects to her first song: "The LORD has seen my misery" (v. 32 NIV).

But in the very next line of the song, Leah switched from acknowledging God's blessing to focusing on the one thing her heart still desired most. She said, "Surely my husband will love me now" (v. 32). Yes, God had seen her struggle, but for Leah, this was only a means to the end of being seen, known, and loved by her husband.

Leah named her second son Simeon, this time declaring, "Because the LORD has heard that I am hated, he has given me this son also" (v. 33 ESV). Leah experienced God seeing and hearing her, but her focus was still on her unchanging circumstances. Her longing for the love of her husband was still louder than her praise.

We see this even more in the name she gave her next son. Levi means "attached" or "connected." When she named Levi, Leah said, "Now this time my husband will be attached to me" (v. 34 ESV).

Unwavering in her determination to win her husband's love, Leah reminds us of something truly important here: when we don't have the one thing we think will make everything better, we are not content with anything.

In ancient Jewish culture, having children was a woman's crowning glory. Not only did children ensure the continuation of the family, but they also grew up to carry on the work of their parents on their land. The fact that God made sure it was Leah who gave Jacob his first three sons would ordinarily have brought joy and confidence to a wife. But because she didn't have the love she longed for from her husband, no gift from God, not even sons, could satisfy Leah's ache.

Besides the cultural importance of having sons, we're told that God gave Leah these sons because He saw her misery, and in her first two proclamations, we hear Leah acknowledge that her sons had come from the Lord. But when we're longing for what we think we must have in order to survive, even the love and blessing of the God of the universe are not enough. Leah was more desperate for a change in the circumstances that caused her misery than she was moved by God's loving attention to the details of her life.

However, something changed for Leah after the birth of Levi. This boy, whom she hoped would attach Jacob to her, apparently didn't. But when Leah gave birth to Judah, her fourth son, she sang a completely different song: "This time I will praise the LORD" (v. 35). The name Judah means "Let God be praised."

As Leah continued to take notice and proclaim that the Lord was blessing her—even though her heart was still set on how she could parlay those blessings into Jacob's acceptance and love—God's faithfulness took root in her heart. She understood that the God of creation saw, knew, and loved her. He was the faithful and constant One relentlessly caring for her. When this truth became her reality, Leah turned fully to Him in hope and with undivided praise.

Her circumstances were unchanged—her husband still didn't love her—but her heart was changed. When Judah was born, Leah lifted her gaze from the thing she didn't have to the One she did have, the One who would love her and carry her through every situation.[1]

Half-Hearted Songs

Upon a first reading, it may not seem like we sing "songs" like Leah's, but we do. So often, God provides in astounding ways, yet after our mumbled prayers of thankfulness, we look at His gifts as means to our own ends.

One of the gifts I'm so thankful for is music. As a child, I processed everything I was learning through songs; they were my prayers of praise and longing. I didn't often share these songs with others, but that changed when I was sixteen.

Having recently joined the youth group at a large church, I somehow worked up the nerve to audition for the youth worship team. The song I auditioned with was one I had written. Our youth leader liked it and asked whether I had written more, so I shared a few. Not only did I make the team, but I was also regularly asked to sing my songs during our Wednesday meetings.

Singing for several hundred kids was terrifying but also gratifying. It opened doors I hadn't expected—namely, I quickly realized that music could help me connect with a roomful of people I couldn't see. It seemed to diminish the barrier between them, the supposed "normal" people, and me, the girl with a "physical challenge." Kids heard in my lyrics their own stories and struggles and felt like I might just be one of them after all. Suddenly my goal of belonging seemed within reach.

I poured myself into my music, but for many wrong reasons. I sang to praise God but also to find a place for myself among my peers. I proclaimed that we are defined by the love of God, not how others value us, yet singing brought me a feeling of self-worth, usefulness, and even power over my circumstances. I sang all through high school and college, and when I signed a record deal a year after graduation, I thought I was finally on the path toward a life of true belonging.

I became a sing-aholic—I said yes to every gig and every interview. I worked on building my career all day, every day. Everyone admired my work ethic. But the magic came at a cost. I was singing to find satisfaction, yet I was anxious. My diet wasn't great, and I rarely slept well. I had little time for meaningful involvement with my friends and church back home. I became increasingly driven by my work, convinced that if things didn't go well, I'd be forced to return to the sidelines, unseen and unknown once again.

I barely noticed how sacrificing my personal life in pursuit of the one thing I thought I needed was taking its toll on my soul. I had turned God's gift of music into a means to an end, and the outcome wasn't good. But God would not leave me to live with my choices forever.

Shifting Desires

Though we don't have to share husbands, as Leah did—or even get married—we still have many things in common with her. We know what it is to have difficult, unchangeable circumstances. We know what it is to feel that if we just had "X," everything would be better. We have all tried in vain to fill the void in our lives, ignoring time and again the One who can actually fill it. We are not convinced that He could ever be enough.

We can learn from Leah what to do about this void: we can praise. We can sing the truth of what God has done for us over and over, until it sinks in. The more we praise, the more our eyes are opened to the beauty, power, and deep love of our Creator. The more we sing to Him of the voids in our lives, the more He fills them with Himself.

Just as He worked in Leah's heart, God worked in mine. When my eight or so years of career hyperfocus inevitably led to burnout, I decided I needed a change of scenery. I moved to New York City for a summer. During that season, I was reawakened to God's unwavering love.

It began with visiting a church. I found that they—and other churches in the area—could use some extra worship leaders. So when I was in town, I spent my Sunday mornings with my new church community and the rest of Sunday helping with music at other local churches.

Attending church in New York City was very different from the large church entities I was used to in the Bible Belt. These NYC churches met in rented buildings, many of which didn't have air-conditioning. There was often no childcare. But nearly all the people I met were intentional in their pursuit of God and relationships with other believers, despite the fact that their faith was culturally unacceptable.

In New York I found myself immersed in true, consistent community for the first time in a long time. As I showed up each week to learn about God, sing to God, and see God in the lives of the folks around me, I began to understand my own desperate need for His love and to realize I could not live a fulfilled life unless He was at the center of it.

I began to talk to God as honestly as I talked to my new friends. I told Him about my burnout. I asked for forgiveness for choosing

my career over Him. And I prayed for true heart change. I started
learning to praise God not merely for the things He had blessed me
with and what they might lead to but simply because of who He is.

My attitude about my career began to change too. I started to
see that music was a gift I'd been given, not so I could find belonging
but so I could bring hope to listeners and praise to the One who
had given that gift. When music became my praise to Him instead
of a means to an end, it brought joy I hadn't felt in years. I began
to experience the beautiful reality that when my heart was full of
gratitude and praise to the Lord, I spent my life responding to Him
instead of longing for what I didn't have.

Like Leah, the "X" I'd been searching for hadn't come. My situ-
ation hadn't changed. But my heart had changed, and now I was
coming alive to the One whose love had been there all along.

The Bigger Story

Leah's struggles didn't end after the birth of Judah. She often returned
to her longing for love from her husband and her competition with her
sister. Though we can hope her life was also characterized by praise to
God, we hear instead how she plotted to win on her own terms.

Leah's bitterness is a reminder that praise is meant to be not
a one-time experience but a constant practice. It should be second
nature for us. The thing we're eager to do as often as we breathe. Not
only is it the joyful outflow of our gratitude for what God has given
us; praise also firmly roots our confidence in Him, even when we
can't see how He will work in our circumstances.

Leah had no idea, when she named her fourth son in unquali-
fied praise of God, that his descendants would become the most

powerful and respected tribe of Israel. Not only that, but it was also from Judah's line that Jesus would one day be born. The God whom Leah praised would come and walk among us, rescuing us from darkness because He wanted us with Him. And for this reason, we praise Him here in the twenty-first century and look back in awe at the plight and the songs of His ancestor Leah.

With this assurance that God has always seen and has always worked behind the scenes, we can look with hope at our own lives. What I didn't know when I lived in New York City for that brief summer was that I'd be moving back there almost a decade later—to stay. And I didn't know that, instead of struggling with a heart overwhelmed with anxiety and burnout, I would be full of hope. I've joined one of the churches where many of my past New York friends attended, and I began working on a master of biblical studies at seminary.

But as fabulously adventurous as it is to live in the big city, it has its challenges. I have started over in a brand-new place. Building friendships and learning the ropes will take time. And besides my full-time career, I'm now also a student tackling twenty-page papers and final exams in highly academically rigorous classes. There are moments when I'm tempted to slip into my old ways—to be defined by how others see me and to become driven again to earn their acceptance.

But when I practice praise, my need to prove myself fades into the background. I've come to see God not only as the giver of blessings that make life great but also as the peace and hope I can't live without. He has begun taking the place of that old desire to receive affirmation from work or the people around me. The more I sing to God and to myself of His constant love and acceptance, the more I can accept and love others, regardless of whether they accept me.

I know my circumstances will not change. I'll always be blind this side of heaven, and that will always make fitting in difficult. But I know that my deep desire to belong is not the be-all and end-all. God is. I will praise Him, in full confidence that I am a tiny part of His greater story.

Even more amazing is the awe-inspiring fact that we are God's desire. Jesus came to earth to forever connect Himself to us, to give us full life (John 10:10). When the Pharisees complained because Jesus was welcoming the broken and empty, He told them that all of heaven rejoices more over one sinner who repents than ninety-nine righteous people who don't need repentance (see Luke 15:1–7). In other words, you and I are the one thing Jesus did not have in heaven, so He came for us.

We can finally change when we begin to accept God's unconditional love for us. When we understand the truth that we are God's desire and that He gives us the undeserved gifts of His love and fellowship, we can't help but overflow with praise. As one author put it, "make God the all of your heart, the one object of your desire."[2]

King David once sang, "I have asked one thing from the LORD; it is what I desire: to dwell in the house of the LORD all the days of my life, gazing on the beauty of the LORD and seeking him in his temple" (Ps. 27:4).

David wanted one thing: to be with God, the author and lover of his soul. Not merely to receive the good things His hand could offer, but to know Him. To experience His presence. When we praise God, our belief grows that we can find all we need in Him, no matter our circumstances.

For me, it means I feel the weight of my deep desire to belong fall away. And when I hear what He says about Himself and about me, my praise becomes an empowering, life-giving song of freedom and deep contentment. It is with real hope that I can happily say, "I am seen, known, and so loved by the God of all." And that is the only "one thing" I really need.

Your Song of Praise

In every chapter of this book, there will be a place for you to write your own song. Now, don't freak out. There are no rules to follow in this process, and you don't have to share with anyone if you don't want to. The point here is to pour out your heart to the Lord. Sing to God with the passion and enthusiasm with which you'd sing your favorite songs. These songs are your declarations of praise, thanksgiving, lament, or request. They can take the form of a literal song or a prayer, letter, poem, or journal entry. The key is to write out words that express how your heart is responding to what we've explored.

Consider where Leah's story intersects with yours. Just as Leah learned to praise God for being God, despite her dark circumstances, I encourage you to praise Him. Start by thinking of some of God's qualities. Describe how God has helped you, impressed you, or stirred you. Jot down words and phrases you think of when you think about God. Pray over those words, and then write your song of praise below. I'll share one of my songs to spur your creativity:

You alone came to free us.
You alone can redeem us.
You are faithful to complete us.
God, You alone.
For Your goodness, we thank You.
For Your greatness, we praise You.[3]

Singing God's Song

Though Leah's song of praise is simple, I think it is useful to memorize it. That way, when we reflect back, we can remember what she was missing and how God gave her peace in spite of it: **"She conceived again, gave birth to a son, and said, 'This time I will praise the LORD'" (Gen. 29:35).**

King David, Leah's distant grandson, proclaimed his desire to know the Lord in Psalm 27. Let's memorize these words too: **"I have asked one thing from the LORD; it is what I desire: to dwell in the house of the LORD all the days of my life, gazing on the beauty of the LORD and seeking him in his temple" (v. 4).**

Listen, you heavens, and I will speak; hear, you earth, the words of my mouth.

Let my teaching fall like rain and my words descend like dew, like showers on new grass, like abundant rain on tender plants.

I will proclaim the name of the LORD. Oh, praise the greatness of our God!

He is the Rock, his works are perfect, and all his ways are just. A faithful God who does no wrong, upright and just is he....

Is this the way you repay the LORD, you foolish and unwise people? Is he not your Father, your Creator, who made you and formed you?...

For the LORD's portion is his people, Jacob his allotted inheritance....

He shielded him and cared for him; he guarded him as the apple of his eye....

The LORD alone led him; no foreign god was with him....

You deserted the Rock, who fathered you; you forgot the God who gave you birth....

"See now that I myself am he! There is no god besides me. I put to death and I bring to life, I have wounded and I will heal, and no one can deliver out of my hand."

Deuteronomy 32:1–4, 6, 9–10, 12, 18, 39 NIV

Chapter 2

A Song for the Plodding Path

The Long, Hard Slog to Nowhere

A few months before I lost my eyesight, a piano came to live at our house. A beaten-up, old, out-of-tune, reddish-oak upright piano. It no longer played well enough to be of use at our church, so instead of ending up on the trash heap, it became my greatest treasure. I quickly discovered I could plunk out my favorite melodies on its ancient keys. I would spend hours finding the notes of familiar songs until I'd play myself to sleep, my three-year-old face squashed against the ivories.

A couple of years into my incessant repetition of the songs I knew from preschool and Sunday school, my mom decided it was time I began piano lessons. I could hardly wait. But sometime during the first lesson, I realized studying piano was not going to be easy. I didn't have the patience to sit still and straight for a half hour of learning scales and proper fingering and memorizing intricate pieces of music. I still don't.

Because I couldn't master every skill immediately, I spent many of my early lessons thinking, *I can see no point in all this monotonous toil.* But because God has a sense of humor, I muddled through a piano lesson nearly every week of my existence until I graduated from college. I came to respect the process, but getting better at piano was—and still is—tedious, grueling work. But God is creatively working behind the scenes, even when we don't see it. As a kid laboring through my practice sessions, I began to experiment with making my own melodies. Soon enough, instead of rehearsing Minuet in G, I was composing full songs.

Since then, writing songs has been my way of journaling—whether as a girl declaring the woes of school life or as a grown-up contemplating the great mysteries. But what I've learned is that songwriting is a slog. Trying to find just the right lyrics and melody to express an idea can take days, months, sometimes years. And once the song is finished and I share it, there is always a chance it will fall flat. And then it's back to the drawing board.

The instrument-learning and songwriting processes are not unlike life. When our efforts pay off, we revel in the results. But what about when they don't? What about when we feel stuck, going through the motions but never moving forward? How can we be satisfied with our lives when they seem to be going nowhere? What do you do when life feels like a never-ending plod?

The Power of the Plod

Perhaps you've found yourself in a season where the work is tedious and monotonous. Perhaps, even though you know in theory that you must be in a time of preparation, you're not quite sure for what or why you're seemingly stuck in your current moment. You're aching for the future to hurry up and get here already.

No matter where we are in life, there is likely some aspect where we feel we're slogging through. Maybe it's a job that isn't fulfilling, a relationship that always feels like work, or simply the pervasive longing for more that never lets up.

Most of us have tried to get unstuck by doing what we can to shake things up—changing jobs, changing relationships, changing our hair.

We try talking to God about our struggles. And if we're honest, it doesn't help. We often feel like our time with Him is itself stuck in a rut. We go through the motions, but they don't change us. So our lives remain tedious or just plain ordinary.

But what if there is true magnificence to be found in the mundane? What if it is on our plodding paths that we find our purpose? What if the God of the universe desires to meet us on the road seemingly headed nowhere, to empower us with strength and dazzle our hearts and eyes with Himself?

The Scriptures are packed with people on plodding paths—called to slog through tedious or difficult circumstances day after day, year after year. Moses is an exceptional example and a wonderful guide on such a journey. He traded one dull phase of his life—a forty-year career of plodding after sheep—for a more difficult season of plodding: leading hundreds of thousands of cranky, clamoring Israelites on a forty-year journey to God's promised place for them.

The Israelites, the people over whom God had given Moses charge, were on their own plodding journey. They had been slaves in Egypt for four hundred years. Then they were wanderers in the desert for another forty.

The story of Moses's transformation as God guided him in the
long game is truly riveting. As the Lord led him one slow, plod-
ding step at a time, his dependence on God grew. He came to see
things more as God sees them. His patience deepened. He became
infinitely wiser and extraordinarily compassionate and loving.

Moses learned quickly how to trust God on his plodding path;
the Israelites were more like me—they had moments of finding their
strength in the One who had ordained their journey, but they typi-
cally forgot God. At the end of his life, the shepherd Moses (who had
once been afraid to speak) sang to the Israelites a song for their plod-
ding path—their new national anthem (see Deut. 32). If it became
the song they loved to sing, its truths would guide them in all the
terrain ahead, long after he had gone.[1]

If we summarized the song of Moses into a song we could
remember, it might go like this:

> *Rehearse God's greatness.*
> *Remember His faithfulness.*
> *Return from darkness.*
> *(Repeat)*

In my mind, this summary song sounds like Moses's rhythm
of walking with God—plodding along, one foot after the other. He
insisted Israel adopt the same walk.

Let's explore Moses's song together to discover what he knew
about singing on every step of the journey—whether delightful or
dull, an easy walk or a laborious crawl. I will also share some of the
miraculous ways God has taught me to sing of hope in the most
mundane moments of my journey.

Rehearse God's Greatness

Moses began his song by calling on the heavens and earth to pay attention, then launched into praising God for His greatness, insisting Israel do the same: "I will proclaim the name of the LORD. Oh, praise the greatness of our God! He is the Rock, his works are perfect, and all his ways are just. A faithful God who does no wrong, upright and just is he" (Deut. 32:3–4 NIV).

Moses knew firsthand of what he sang, as did his people. They'd witnessed God's greatness as He brought plagues, which disproved the existence of all the Egyptian gods, leaving Pharaoh and his people helpless and Yahweh and His enslaved people victorious (Ex. 7–12). They'd seen God's greatness as He split the Red Sea for them to cross but closed it again over their Egyptian pursuers (Ex. 14). While in the desert, they'd witnessed God's greatness as He led them with a pillar of fire and a cloud and protected them from the attack of surrounding nations, who could have instantly wiped them out (Num. 14:14). God's great power and strength had also come against them when they had ignored His instruction and chosen their own path—railing against Him and worshipping idols (Ex. 32; Num. 11:1–3).

Moses was teaching the Israelites to drill God's greatness into their minds until they believed it. And why? It wasn't another ritual to add to their religious practices; it was to inspire their love, wonder, and confidence in who He is. It was to convince them that God is God and they were not. It was so that whenever they faced circumstances they did not understand—whether uncertain, adverse, or monotonous—they would run to their great God. Moses knew that if Israel sang to their own hearts and to one another of God's greatness, it would change them into people who centered their lives on Him.

The Practice of Singing God's Greatness

As we discovered in the last chapter, when our hearts are not tuned to sing God's praise, our sense of His awesomeness and power fades away. We get overwhelmed by the cares of the world, the holding pattern we're in, and the fact that life is not going according to plan. We try to take on the role of God, believing that the steps ahead are up to us. But eventually our inability to do what God can do frustrates and angers us and leaves us feeling more stuck than ever.

Singing of God's greatness empowers and renews us in the truth that there is a perfect, holy One worthy of all our love and worship—One who loves us so much He would come to save us and walk with us through every moment.

I remember a season when I began to learn of God's greatness firsthand. My playing and songwriting had led me to Belmont University, a school in Nashville known for its outstanding music program. I loved the idea of making music for a living, but I also knew that was not necessarily practical, so I spent three years in a double major of commercial vocal performance and music education. But at the end of my junior year, when I auditioned for the hundredth time for one of the music school's elite ensembles and, for the hundredth time, failed to get in, my professor said something that changed everything.

"Ginny, your voice is just weak," she bluntly explained. "It's unrealistic to think you'll be able to make a career out of using it."

I was hurt by her words, but I knew they weren't meant to be hurtful. So I cut the cord of the dangling dream to write and sing. I dropped my performance major and threw myself headlong into finishing my music ed degree. This meant I spent my next semester taking all the general education classes I'd been putting off while focusing on my music coursework.

I thought I was going to die from the workload, to say nothing of sheer boredom. I went to class, came home, did exorbitant amounts of homework for subjects I would never use again, fell into bed in the middle of the night, and did it all again the next day. Most concerning, I could not see the road ahead, and I could only hope against hope that somehow the work would pay off.

But during that semester, I also found myself involved in a college group at a new church I was attending. Our leader was a kind, soft-spoken, middle-aged family man who adored the Lord and taught us what it meant to rehearse His greatness. Each Sunday we would show up to learn about who God is and talk about what it meant to respond to His goodness with our lives. We would then share all our concerns, doubts, and fears, and together we would pray. As our teacher led us in prayer, he modeled what it was to pray with hope and confidence. With God's greatness in focus, we knew He heard us, longed to draw us closer, and would powerfully work in our circumstances.

Moved by all I was learning, I experienced something delightfully unexpected during this desert semester: while sitting in those mundane general ed classes, I wrote more songs than I had during my entire college career, perhaps even my life up to that point. The premise of many of them was the same: *I don't know what You're doing, but I know You are God, and I know You are good. And that is enough.*

I had no idea at the time that this collage of songs would eventually make up much of my first album.

Remember: God's Faithfulness in Uncertainty

In the song Moses taught Israel, nine consecutive verses encourage meditation on God's faithfulness. "Is not [God] your father, who created you, who made you and established you?" (Deut. 32:6 ESV). Moses went on to sing that if the Hebrews asked their fathers, they would tell them of God's history of faithfulness. From His promise to give Abraham and Sarah a son, to protecting Abraham's grandson Jacob from being undone by his foolish mistakes, to preserving Jacob's family through his son, Joseph, who became second-in-command in Egypt despite his brothers' desire to murder him and his unjust imprisonment, God had been faithful. With God's guidance, Joseph anticipated a severe famine, stored up food for the entire nation of Egypt, and moved his family to live there with him. And then, after the Egyptians had enslaved Jacob's family for four hundred years, God had sent Moses to the rescue.

Moses left quite a legacy. In the New Testament, he is referenced by Jesus (Mark 12:26), the apostles (Acts 3:22; 13:39), and the author of Hebrews (11:23–28). Even in modern culture, elements of his story are figures of speech: "parting the Red Sea" and "mass exodus," for example.

But what I love about Moses's story is that he had no idea he was preparing for a life that would leave a legacy. It was in the dullness, in the plodding, that he became "the man of God" (Deut. 33:1). His story encourages us all that plodding down a path that feels mundane might be the most glorious choice we can make.

Moses, you might remember, was rescued at three months old from the genocide that Pharaoh, the Egyptian king, was perpetrating against Israelite baby boys. One of Pharaoh's daughters found him in a basket in the Nile River and took him to live in the royal palace, adopting him as her son (Ex. 2:1–10).

Instead of laboring in the hot sun, making bricks with the rest of his people, Moses was a "silver spoon" kid, receiving everything an Egyptian prince got, including a first-class education (Acts 7:22). Moses came of age destined for greatness. But his heart was stirred as he realized that beyond his ornate palace walls, his people were being abused.

One day, around the ripe young age of forty, Moses saw one of his fellow Jews being wronged, and "he defended the oppressed man and avenged him by striking down the Egyptian" (vv. 23–24 ESV). Again, we hear the Bible speaking the truth as it was. In Moses's time, avenging someone with murder would have been more culturally acceptable than it is now, though not acceptable in God's sight.

Moses thought "his brothers would understand that God was giving them salvation by his hand" (v. 25 ESV), but after the murder, his people openly rejected him (vv. 27–28), and Pharaoh set out to kill him (Ex. 2:15).

Moses escaped to the desert of Midian (in the west of what is modern-day Saudi Arabia), where he married a priest's daughter. Then he began tending his father-in-law's sheep, a job he held for roughly forty years (Ex. 2:15–21; Acts 7:30).

Can you imagine the utter dullness? The man prepared for power as a prince presided not over people or governmental matters, but over sheep. Yet God had protected him from death twice, and little did Moses know, God had an elaborate plan prepared for his future.

Remember: God's Faithfulness in Every Detail

I've often wondered what it must have been like for Moses, that prince, scholar, and bold proponent of justice turned outlaw turned shepherd. He was probably resigned to the idea that he would spend the rest of his life sheep-tending in the desert. But at eighty, at the point when most folks are slowing down, God came to Moses, singing of the detour that would become his new road.

God interrupted Moses's ordinary day with a burning bush that did not burn up and explained His reason for this meeting:

> I am the God of your father.... I have observed the misery of my people in Egypt, and have heard them crying out because of their oppressors.... I have come down to rescue them from the power of the Egyptians and to bring them from that land to a good and spacious land, a land flowing with milk and honey. (Ex. 3:6–8)

And then came the clincher—God told Moses he would be the one to do the legwork: "Therefore, go. I am sending you to Pharaoh so that you may lead my people, the Israelites, out of Egypt" (v. 10).

For four hundred years, the Israelites had prayed for this day to come. But Moses was undoubtedly shocked that the Lord was there then, telling *him*. He was definitely not ready for what God had in mind.

"Who am I that I should go?" he asked (v. 11).

In answer, God introduced a concept that Moses would come to understand firsthand: "I will certainly be with you" (v. 12). In other words, "It isn't about who you are, Moses—it's about who I am. I am God, and I am with you."

God always gives us *Himself* as the answer to our fears and questions, reminding us that when He calls us to walk through a dark season or to do a difficult thing, He never asks us to do it in our own strength. He insists we do it in His.

Moses continued to question God, which is perfectly understandable. After years of herding sheep, he probably doubted his ability to lead people. And he almost certainly did not possess the courage to speak to a king. Moses seemed certain that his dull life was better than God's extraordinary plan. God's plan would mean heading in a new direction, where only God knew the way. It would require trust.

But Moses did get one thing most of us don't usually get: a clear picture of what would happen next. God commanded Moses to tell the people that He had sent him to them. He would bring them out of Egypt to the Promised Land. God even said that the people would listen (vv. 15–18). Then He gave Moses precise instructions and a description of what was to come (vv. 18–22):

> 1. He was to ask Pharaoh to let his people go into the desert to worship.
> 2. Pharaoh wouldn't let them go … until the Lord struck Egypt with all His miracles.
> 3. Then the people would go, with the Egyptians willingly giving them their treasures.

The God of all had thought of everything, but Moses still questioned Him further: "What if they won't believe me and will not obey me but say, 'The LORD did not appear to you'?" (4:1).

We might at first wonder how Moses could argue with the God of his fathers, who was speaking to him from a fire. At this point, though, Moses's fear was greater than his faith. He remembered his people's rejection of him, which led to a forty-year estrangement. But the Lord empowered Moses by repeatedly showing His faithfulness until it was the rhythm he learned to trust.

Remember: God's Faithful Leading

God, in his graciousness, answered Moses's declaration of doubt with a question.

> The LORD asked him, "What is that in your hand?"
> "A staff," he replied.
> "Throw it on the ground," he said. So Moses threw it on the ground, it became a snake, and he ran from it. (4:2–3)

The Lord didn't coddle Moses but invited him to face his fear by commanding him to pick up the snake by the tail. Moses did so, and it became a staff again. The Lord explained that Moses would use this sign to convince the Israelites that the God of their fathers had indeed appeared to him (vv. 4–5).

In that moment, God began teaching Moses to trust that He is faithful. But even after God discussed with Moses two more signs he would use with Pharaoh, Moses was still not convinced. His last-ditch effort to avoid this task was to use the excuse that he couldn't speak well (v. 10).

God responded with an astounding declaration: "Who has made man's mouth? Who makes him mute, or deaf, or seeing, or blind? Is it not I, the LORD? Now therefore go, and I will be with your mouth and teach you what you shall speak" (vv. 11–12 ESV).

An incredible challenge when we are facing darkness—whether that darkness be a season of feeling stuck or lost or wondering where God is—is to trust that God has allowed the darkness in our lives and will faithfully guide us through it.

Sure, our sin or other people's sin can be the catalyst. And yes, the evils of the world can unfairly fall on us. But as Joni Eareckson Tada has said, "Satan and God may want the exact same event to take place—but for different reasons."[2]

God absolutely does not delight in our pain. And He is always right there in the midst of it with us, working all things together for good (Rom. 8:28). Even when we don't understand why things aren't going according to our plans, we can be confident that the Lord is always faithfully offering His unwavering strength to us.

When I graduated university armed with a teaching license, I had an extraordinary plan for my life:

1. Become an exceptional, well-loved choral director.
2. Help students love both classical and current music.
3. Perhaps get a few of my songs sung by professionals.

I sent out résumés and applications so I could quickly get this plan on the road. A few school administrators got in touch to say they'd like an interview. I was ecstatic. But based on the awkward silence upon meeting each principal, I realized that not being able to see was going to be a greater hurdle than I had anticipated. I tried addressing the questions they wouldn't ask, like how I'd manage a classroom. But nothing worked.

I met one closed door after another.

At first I believed God was testing me or teaching me patience or instilling some other character trait I'd recognize later. But after several months of interviews, I was just frustrated. God was not going along with my extraordinary plan. I was thankful for the full-time telemarketing job I'd managed to land, but it wasn't exactly what I had pictured myself doing after graduation. I was completely over the mundaneness of it all.

Where had I gone wrong? I had given up on my music dream, and now my plan to teach was not panning out either? Every day was a plod. I wasn't sure where I was headed. And I didn't know where God was.

Yet, having had God's answer to Moses in Exodus 4:11 in my mind since childhood, I knew God had not made a mistake. Whether I saw it or not, He had an infinite purpose for my "stuckness" and lack of job prospects in my field of study.

During my season of limbo, I began to ask God to show me how to trust that He had some purpose to this detour—and He did. What I believed about God began to change—slowly at first but then drastically.

Through talking life out with mentors and digging deeply into the Scriptures, I discovered that grace was not favor I earned from God by behaving a certain way but God giving Himself freely to me. As I began to recognize that I was God's dearly beloved daughter, I was able to look back and see how He had already proved this time and again. This truth was so life changing for me that it prompted new songs, which I would eventually share with audiences. It became clear in that season that my tedious plodding was God's good plan.

We often stop believing that God is good because we don't see eye to eye with Him on what good *is*. We think that when something is difficult, God is not in control, has gotten it wrong, or doesn't care. As I went to Him with my questions and as I asked Him for peace, He began to show me who He was in ways I'd never seen. As I waited for something extraordinary to happen, I began to realize that the extraordinary One was walking with me. He was eager to give me new eyes to see the dull, plodding path as a road full of vibrant colors and awesome wonders.

As Moses taught the Israelites to sing their national anthem, he surely remembered the first day when God came to him and gave power to his shepherd's staff. And he wanted them to remember God's faithfulness as He provided a cloud and a pillar for guidance, food and water in the wilderness, protection from enemies, and laws of justice and mercy to guide them.

Remembering God's faithfulness, Moses no doubt taught Israel to sing with all fervor and gusto: "The LORD's portion is his people, Jacob his allotted inheritance. In a desert land he found him, in a barren and howling waste. He shielded him and cared for him; he guarded him as the apple of his eye.... The LORD alone led him" (Deut. 32:9–10, 12 NIV).

Return from Darkness

Much of the song Moses taught the Israelites is about what would happen when they turned away from God. During his forty-year journey with them, he watched them reject God over and over. He knew they would again.

When God delivered His people from Egypt, He led them away with treasures given to them by the Egyptians, and He provided guidance and protection on their way. But as soon as Israel realized Pharaoh and his army were pursuing them, they lost it—yelling at Moses for not leaving them enslaved, a more preferable situation to the death they thought was imminent (Ex. 14:11–12). But then, through Moses, the Lord parted the sea, saving the Hebrews and thwarting the Egyptian ambush.

The Israelites were thankful at first, praising God with an ecstatic song of gratitude for their rescue (15:1–21). But only three days later, they were grumbling again because they could not find water in the wilderness (v. 24). Moses immediately cried to the Lord for help, and God provided (v. 25). This rhythm repeated throughout the rest of Moses's life: he trusted God to lead the way, the people grumbled against him and God, Moses desperately pleaded with God for mercy, and God delivered them.

Three months after their departure from Egypt, the Lord prepared to give Moses the laws that would protect Israel in the desert and when they were settled as a nation. The people promised with one accord to do all that the Lord said (19:8). Then Moses brought the people to meet with God. They heard the loud trumpet and saw Mount Sinai engulfed with God's fire. They were terrified and begged Moses to be the one to listen to and speak with God; they were too afraid (19:17–20; 20:18–19).

How quickly they forgot what they had seen and heard! When Moses went up for an extended meeting with God on Mount Sinai, Israel had Aaron, the priest, make them a golden god to serve (32:1–6). The entire rest of the Old Testament is about the Israelites' tendency to rebel against the Lord their God and follow other gods, as God and Moses knew they would. The words of their national anthem were to remind them both of their predisposition to run from God and of their desperate need to turn to Him again.

I have come to learn something that Moses knew well: Any path you take in your own strength, no matter how adventurous at first, will eventually feel endlessly monotonous and become dangerous. But leaning fully on God's faithfulness brings you strength and hope, whatever road He is leading you on.

Within a year of starting to find purpose in my own plodding path, I was recording my first album as a solo artist. A music publisher in town had heard some of my homegrown songs and revived my dormant singing dream. The songs I had written during my semester of general education classes were some of his favorites, and after they were tweaked, those songs—and their writer—found a home at Michael W. Smith's new record label, Rocketown Records.

As all this came into view, my excitement grew in leaps and bounds. When my record released, I quit my day job to venture out into the world of touring. My extraordinary life had finally arrived.

Six months in, however, I was over it.

Each day was long and filled with endless work—traveling, interviews, and marketing meetings. I did very little actual singing and even less communing with God. Like the Israelites, I began to forget what it was like to wait for His wisdom and find His rest.

I turned to other gods—my career and pleasing others. I learned there is no such thing as living in a neutral place. We are always moving in a direction. And if the noise of our lives is pulling us away from the light of God's love and truth, our only hope is to return from the darkness. My inner peace, my ability to navigate the stress of my new life, did not return until I turned my gaze back to God.

Repeat

Despite my disenchantment, my early years of piano practice, songwriting, and incessant touring helped me flourish. I learned to patiently craft songs, to sing without stage fright, and to love meeting new people. I also began to learn in that season something I'm grasping even more deeply now: putting in the work pays off. Because of all that work, today I am able to sing in any type of situation and under any kind of pressure.

But beyond literal singing, I've learned that my *heart* sings only when I'm not trying to forge this path on my own. When I'm holding tightly to the hand of my Father, listening to His voice for guidance, I'm content with putting one foot in front of the other on this faith walk, no matter how fast or slow the pace. I'm a more peaceful and loving child of His and friend to others when I sing along with the essence of Moses's song:

Rehearse God's greatness.
Remember His faithfulness.
Return from darkness.
(Repeat)

The Bigger Story

I love that God was preparing Moses for his world-changing adventures throughout every moment of his plodding life beforehand. Moses needed his education to write the Pentateuch, the first five books of the Bible. He needed his military training for leadership and logistics. And he needed his shepherding skills so he could patiently protect and manage the people God had tasked him with.

Moses also learned to truly love the intractable people God had entrusted to him, leading, disciplining, and challenging them in a way he could not have done as a young man. But as a man fully resting in God's guidance, he could.

Moses points us toward Jesus, who spent His life on earth serving, loving, listening, speaking truth, and trusting His Father—and repeating those actions again and again. But Moses could not do all that Christ did. Moses's plodding path under God's leadership led the Israelites to the borders of the Promised Land. Christ's plodding path led Him to the cross we should have carried. As we grumbled, like the children of Israel grumbled, Jesus quietly, humbly, powerfully led us into ultimate and lasting freedom—once and for all.

When my career, whether teaching or music, was my only goal at the end of the plodding path, it felt mundane. I wanted to get there in a hurry, to accomplish all my goals yesterday. Indeed, the things I have accomplished have been greatly rewarding—for at least a few hours. But when they matter to me more than anything else, the next morning is always a grind all over again.

But when my goal is walking with God on the plodding path, it feels life-giving. There is opportunity to stop and enjoy the beauty of nature or time with a friend. There is space for listening, breathing, and praying. And there's lots of singing of hope as I go—step by step by step.

Your Song for the Plodding Path

Where are you in your journey? Do you feel as if God has you on an endless, ordinary road and you don't know why? Do you feel like the pathway is so full of busyness that you can't find God's hand or hear His voice? Or perhaps the pace you're keeping is a peaceful plod onward.

Wherever you are, write a song for your path below. Here are some words to inspire you:

> *Be Thou my vision,*
> *O Lord of my heart;*
> *Naught be all else to me,*
> *Save that Thou art—*
> *Thou my best thought*
> *By day or by night,*
> *Waking or sleeping,*
> *Thy presence my light.*[3]

Singing God's Song

Let's sing and remember God's faithfulness, just as Moses and Israel did: *"He is the Rock, his works are perfect, and all his ways are just. A faithful God who does no wrong, upright and just is he"* *(Deut. 32:4 NIV).*

Centuries later, when the Israelites had forgotten the truth of their national anthem for long enough, they were exiled from the Promised Land. Still, the Lord promised that if they would turn again to Him, He would be found by them. He promises this hope to us too. So let's memorize these words: *"You will seek me and find me when you search for me with all your heart" (Jer. 29:13).*

On that day Deborah and Barak son of Abinoam sang:

When the leaders lead in Israel, when the people volunteer, blessed be the LORD. Listen, kings! Pay attention, princes! I will sing to the LORD; I will sing praise to the LORD God of Israel. LORD, when you came from Seir, when you marched from the fields of Edom, the earth trembled, the skies poured rain, and the clouds poured water. The mountains melted before the LORD, even Sinai, before the LORD, the God of Israel.

In the days of Shamgar son of Anath, in the days of Jael, the main roads were deserted because travelers kept to the side roads. Villages were deserted, they were deserted in Israel, until I, Deborah, arose, a mother in Israel. Israel chose new gods, then there was war in the city gates. Not a shield or spear was seen among forty thousand in Israel. My heart is with the leaders of Israel, with the volunteers of the people. Blessed be the LORD! You who ride on white donkeys, who sit on saddle blankets, and who travel on the road, give praise! Let them tell the righteous acts of the LORD, the righteous deeds of his villagers in Israel, with the voices of the singers at the watering places. Then the LORD's people went down to the city gates. "Awake! Awake, Deborah! Awake! Awake, sing a song! Arise, Barak, and take your prisoners, son of Abinoam!"...

The stars fought from the heavens; the stars fought with Sisera from their paths. The river Kishon swept them away, the ancient river, the river Kishon. March on, my soul, in strength!

Judges 5:1–12, 20–21

Chapter 3

A Song of Victory

Storm Songs

I am pretty sure I was born with music in my bones. My mom says I used to leap in utero any time the choir sang at church or when she and Dad played their Karen Carpenter and ABBA records. And once I was out of the womb, all bets were off. My parents have enjoyed recounting the details of when I, a bold and brash two-year-old, stood resolute on the front pew before the church choir, insisting they were singing the "Hallelujah Chorus" incorrectly. I then proceeded to demonstrate how it should be sung (horrors!).

Besides singing with my parents' seventies records and torturing poor parishioners, I spent much time in song with my aunt Carol, my mom's younger sister. She was in college when I came along, and I adored being with her. I made frequent visits to her college dorm, and we'd drive around town together, singing along to "Cheeseburger in Paradise" and "Lay Down Sally."

My mom requested that Aunt Carol find some more age-appropriate songs for a preschool music sponge. So she did, adding more educational numbers to our repertoire, including a kids' song her roommate had on vinyl called "Storms." The song was terrifying, with loud, scary thunder booms and torrential-downpour sounds, and lyrics describing every type of storm a kid could imagine. For as many times as she'd agree to it, I'd have Aunt Carol play it, and I would hide under the covers. When the claps of thunder burst forth from the record player, I'd bury my head under her pillow and squeal with terror and delight.

I didn't know it then, but Aunt Carol had written her own share of songs about life's storms. Music was for her a place of peace. She loved singing hymns in church and started creating her own masterpieces in middle school, when she got a ukulele and her big sister (my mom) got a Silvertone guitar. As a teen, Aunt Carol and her musical compadres would play at church, school, and a local home for girls, often singing songs of hope she had journaled during her own dark days.

My path was similar to Aunt Carol's in some ways. As a child, I began to write my own way through life's personal downpours. I would process whatever was going on by going to the piano. Crafting songs of hope in the midst of suffering—mine or others'—grew into a lifelong habit for me.

But I remember one particular season when the songs and the hope behind them dried up. The storm was fierce, and I could not sing my way out of it.

In the early months of 2008, my mom was diagnosed with stage-three breast cancer. We were all blindsided by the news. She would go through multiple rounds of potent chemotherapy with intense side effects. Then surgery. Then more chemo. And finally, radiation.

It was a dark, scary, rotten season. And I, the author of so many hopeful songs, felt my hope and peace ebbing away.

Enter Aunt Carol. Despite her own sadness at the situation, over the next few months she began to teach us victory songs to carry us through the storm. She calls them "cheer songs" these days, though they aren't light and fluffy like the word *cheer* connotes. They are subtly powerful choruses of praise, calling us toward hope in the midst of suffering and doubt.

What does it mean to sing of victory during life's storms? We all find ourselves in darkness from time to time. In fact, I think there's always a low-level storm brewing in our souls. Worry, unrest, and fear threaten our sanity and diminish our joy.

Whether it's a global pandemic, unrest, or rising panic about what the future may hold, the world seems to have a knack for finding ways to throw new fears at us. In the midst of all that noise, it's easy to wonder if God cares and, if so, where He's hiding. It's easy to stop singing because of a storm or the threat of bad weather ahead. How often are we like Peter walking on the water to Jesus, distracted by the wind and the waves and forgetting that he was living in a miracle (Matt. 14:28–33)? But what if we believed that God's victory is always at hand? How would it change us?

Deborah is a powerful woman we meet during a dark season in Israel's history. Her courage and her song of victory remind me of my aunt Carol and her cheer songs. Deborah's song in Judges 5 is one of the oldest pieces of Hebrew poetry we have. In it, Deborah and Barak, her partner in battle, sang about how victory came for them and their nation and how it can come for us too.

Become Who You Already Are

The book of Judges paints a grim picture of the life of the nation of Israel. The people frequently forgot to sing the anthem Moses had taught them. Instead, they were all doing what was right in their own eyes (Judg. 17:6). They were surrounded by Canaanite nations who excelled at unjust and vulgar practices like child sacrifice and temple prostitution. Israel would adopt all their ways at different points in their history, but at this stage in the game, they were very much into worshipping false gods (3:5–7). This practice naturally led them, again and again, to turn their backs on Yahweh.

Whenever they ceased to listen to His voice, they would make stupid choices. This would always result in one of the surrounding Canaanite nations invading them and making their lives miserable. Then God's people would wake up and turn again to Him, crying out for rescue. The Lord would respond by raising up a deliverer to restore the nation's peace. But as soon as Israel once more felt confident and comfortable, they would turn from the Lord again, and the pattern would repeat.

In Judges 4, we find Deborah, a courageous and confident prophetess and judge, presiding over the people of Israel while they were in one of those seasons of turning away from the Lord (v. 1). As a result of their evil, the Lord allowed King Jabin of Canaan, whose army was led by a harsh commander named Sisera, to oppress them for twenty years (v. 3). But when God's people cried out to Him to save them, the Lord heard and engaged Deborah to help bring change.

Despite the heaviness laid on her nation, Deborah's posture was toward the Lord. We don't see her performing strange rituals or calling on other gods, nor do we hear fear or doubt as she navigated her people through this season of oppression. Instead, the fact that she belonged to the Lord is evident. She knew that her identity was in God, and she reminded the people of Israel that theirs was too. When they remembered that, they could become what God's people should be.[1] Deborah's influence led the nation into a season of faithfulness and to victory in a harrowing battle that the Lord won on their behalf.

Deborah began implementing the Lord's battle plan by sending for a man, Barak, and boldly giving him his marching orders (v. 6). Deborah didn't assume the typical place of women in ancient Near Eastern cultures nor the typical attitude of an Israelite toward God. Instead, she shattered stereotypes with her leadership role, her tight connection to the Lord, and her incredible boldness in doing His will.

With utmost confidence, she delivered to Barak the message of the one true God: "The LORD, the God of Israel, commands you, 'Go, take position at Mount Tabor, bringing ten thousand from the tribe of Naphtali and the tribe of Zebulun'" (v. 6 NRSV). The Lord then promised through Deborah to give Sisera, the cruel Canaanite commander, and his massive army into Israel's hands (v. 7).

But Barak was not courageous like Deborah, and because he was too afraid to go to battle without her, she said she'd go but the Lord would give the victory to a woman because of his reluctance (vv. 8–9). Accompanied by Deborah, Barak followed the Lord's orders, gathering troops and preparing for battle (v. 10). Then Deborah, moved by the word of the Lord, gave Barak the order to go and fight: "Up! For this is the day on which the LORD has given Sisera into your hand. The LORD is indeed going out before you" (v. 14 NRSV).

What Deborah and Barak show us here is so important that they led Israel in singing about it. There are only two postures we can assume in life: toward God or away from God. Rooted in Him or rooted in something else. God has created us in His image, to be in communion with Him (Gen. 1:27). But we tend to trust our own abilities and chase after other gods. This failure to trust God naturally separates us from Him (see Gen. 3).

Because Israel belonged to God, He was "slow to anger and abounding in faithful love" (Num. 14:18), forgiving their sins when they ran back to Him. He gave them leaders like Deborah, who lived her life turned toward God. Her identity was rooted in Him. As a result, she had the courage and confidence to lead her people wherever God sent them, even if He called them into a dangerous battle.

For the Israelites, forgetting who they were meant forgetting the Lord. They turned to the worship of physical idols, which is a practice that is unfamiliar to most of us. But we have many idols of our own—many ways we forget or dismiss God.

These days, many folks prefer a combo of religions. Even Christians sometimes cherry-pick the things we like in Christianity, adding Eastern religious ideas like karma and more secular beliefs like self-empowerment. Perhaps our gods are our talents, our wealth, or our children.

Whatever they are, to trust in these gods means that chaos will eventually ensue. We implode when the thing we love most fails us. Or, as anxiety rises about what bad things could happen, we tune out the panic by scrolling through social media or binge-watching instead of taking our doubts, fears, and questions to God and His Word. No matter what course we take away from God, the further we move from Him, the more unmanageable life becomes.

Embracing that we are God's image bearers is the first step we take toward freedom. We were made in His image so we could have connection with Him. He wanted that connection with us so much that He sent His own Son to pay for all our turning away (John

3:16). To belong to Him means to be His children and heirs (Rom. 8:16–17). It means we are no longer wandering orphans, managing life on our own (John 14:18). Finding our identity in Christ is the key to victory in the battles of our lives.

We could have no more beautiful, purposeful, or powerful identity than to be God's children and coheirs with Christ. When we are rooted in Him, we will have an unending sense of purpose and hope even when our circumstances do not change. Our hearts will be in a posture to receive His love and His answers. Our ears will be tuned to the sound of His irresistible song.

The words of Deborah and Barak's song pierce my heart: "When the people offer themselves willingly—bless the LORD!… When new gods were chosen, then war was in the gates" (Judg. 5:2, 8 NRSV).

I wrestled intensely with my mom's cancer diagnosis, partly because of how much I valued stability. I found that stability was one of my idols—and suddenly it was gone. I wanted life to move happily along as normal, uninterrupted. Most of all, I desperately wanted Mom to be okay. The realization that I could take care of her but couldn't fix her cancer left me in a haze of sadness.

Looking back, I realize there were many days when I forgot that my identity was in the Lord. I would not have said I was hostile to Him, but in those times, I did not often seek Him out, which is pretty much the same thing. Instead, I threw myself into helping Mom however I could, and I used whatever fuel I had left on songwriting and keeping my career on the rails. Beyond that, I came up with endless ways to distract myself so I wouldn't have to feel.

Mom, for her part, was getting treatments and then going back to work as many days a week as she could. She and I would pray together and sometimes talk through the hard questions. But there were no answers, so the sadness weighed heavily on us. Enter Aunt Carol. Like Deborah, she led the charge in reminding my mom and me of our identity.

None of us knew what would result from my mom's cancer diagnosis. But in that dark season of uncertainty, Aunt Carol's confidence that we belonged to the Lord and that He would be faithful brought courage. She led us in singing of God's goodness and faithfulness and of our identity as His children. And when we couldn't sing on our own, she sang it over us.

Don't Just Stand There

I think it's incredibly significant that Deborah and Barak chose to include in their song a stanza about those who followed God's call into battle—and those who stood around instead.

Deborah, acting as "a mother in Israel" (Judg. 5:7), faithfully delivered the Lord's orders for battle. Barak faithfully mobilized ten thousand volunteer troops, who willingly marched into battle (4:14; 5:9, 12–15).

Others, however, weren't so willing or faithful. The song tells of the tribe of Reuben, who underwent "great searchings of heart," walking among their sheep instead of going to help (vv. 15–16 ESV). Reuben was thinking about getting involved—apparently thinking about it a lot. We're told twice in the song about their "searchings of heart." But they didn't go. Nor did other tribes like Dan or Asher (v. 17).

Some tribes may not have gone up to fight because of economic alliances with Canaan. Then, as now, it's financially inconvenient to tick off your trade partners. Others probably didn't go because they were fairly far away from where the battle would take place. Still, Deborah and Barak sang severe words of correction for these tribes who thought more about their own interests and well-being than about protecting their brothers and sisters.[2]

Like Deborah, my aunt Carol knew who she was. And like those ten thousand volunteers, she acted on it. When my mom was first diagnosed, Aunt Carol wrote encouraging lyrics to the tunes of favorite kids' songs. To the melody of "Twinkle, Twinkle, Little Star," she wrote:

> *Cancer, cancer, cancer-free—*
> *That is what I'm going to be.*
> *Friendships, loved ones, prayer, and hope,*
> *They're the things to help me cope.*
> *Cancer, cancer, cancer-free—*
> *That is what I'm going to be.*

After a stream of these came in via email, my mom had had enough. It was too soon for enthusiasm. "Can you please stop with the songs?" she begged. "I'm just not in the place for that right now."

Aunt Carol couldn't shirk her call to champion hope, so she came up with a new approach. Thus, cheer songs were born. "Cheer song" was the subject line of every new email that offered a hymn or praise lyric, an encouraging Scripture, a short devotional, or a quick anecdote from Aunt Carol. Cheer songs began showing up in our inboxes without fail every evening. Soon enough, receiving the encouragement of these messages became a favorite part of our day. Mom began sharing them with friends and coworkers, and the list of recipients grew.

I was inspired by my aunt's tenacity. Left to myself, I am more like the tribe of Reuben. I search my heart, pondering for hours and sometimes years all the ways I could take action. Thinking carefully is not a bad thing, of course, unless it ends with not responding to what God has called us to do. But more recently I have discovered what Deborah and her comrades knew: being known and loved by God means we can never live passive lives. Even in the waiting, we listen, we cry out, and we pursue Him and the things He puts in front of us—just as He pursues us.

So often we are paralyzed by fear. We don't move because we don't know what God wants us to do. I've been delighted to learn that we actually do know what He wants us to do—or at least where to begin. And He's been telling us for years. For the Israelites, He carefully laid out the ways His people were to live, and Jesus succinctly summarized them later: "Love the Lord your God with all your heart, with all your soul, and with all your mind.... Love your neighbor as yourself" (Matt. 22:37, 39).

Deborah knew this. As she loved God with all her heart, she trusted and obeyed Him and sought the good of her people. Her trust was contagious. Barak caught on too. Though skittish and fearful at first, he followed Deborah's example. They influenced ten thousand troops to follow suit in defending their fellow Israelites and trusting that God would give them the battle.

So even when we face the unknown, even when we are surrounded by uncertainty, even in the waiting, we have important things to do. We get to entrust our searching hearts to the Lord and to share them with one another. We love as we have been loved. And we continually practice resting our wearied souls in the arms of the only One who can fight our battles and carry us to victory.

The Bigger Story

Deborah and Barak's song celebrates how God's greatness alone won this battle for Israel. Yes, Deborah was faithful. Yes, Barak, though wimpy, did what he was called to do. But think about how much of this story had nothing to do with the Israelites.

First, there is no line in this song about the Israelites having to do the heavy lifting in the battle. Instead, the Canaanites, with their fancy, powerful chariots, were overwhelmed by a storm (Judg. 5:4–5).[3] The Israelites sang of the stars fighting from heaven on their behalf (v. 20). We are told that, in the thick of the battle, "the LORD threw Sisera, all his charioteers, and all his army into a panic" (4:15).

What's more, the Lord used Jael—a non-Israelite, tent-dwelling woman—to courageously defend His people by singlehandedly taking on Sisera (5:24–27). After his army was defeated, Sisera ran from the battle and happened upon Jael's tent. She invited him in, gave him milk, and covered him up for a nap. Then, while he slept, she drove a tent peg into his temple (4:17–21).

What a savage story for our modern ears! It is helpful to remember that God was unleashing justice on a merciless overlord who had abused His people. And He did it through an outsider who "risked everything to execute the enemy of God."[4] Only an all-powerful God could set this plan in motion, making it happen for His glory and the good of His people. As a result, Israel listened to Deborah and Barak's song of victory, renewed in their hope that the battle belongs to God.

God's ways of saving His people are often beautifully mysterious and unexpected. Yet, no matter how faithful the children of Israel saw that He was, they consistently forgot. God had protected and provided for them by freeing them from slavery and leading them safely through the wilderness to the Promised Land. Yet they turned their hearts away.

But in His grace, He rescued them when they cried out for mercy. He took on the Canaanites with the forces of nature, attacking with a ferocity and strength that Israel could not muster on its own and did not deserve. He sent a storm to overpower their enemy and a woman with a tent peg to take down their cruel overlord.

Throughout Israel's remaining time in the Promised Land, God sent judges and kings to protect and lead His people. And they repeatedly turned from Him. Finally, He sent His Son, who, in an act of unbelievable power and humility, laid down His life on a cross, winning the ultimate victory of eternal life and freedom for all who believe.

Now we wait for Jesus to return and to give us, as Paul said, incorruptible bodies and victory over death once and for all. Paul's song explodes as he talked about this: "Thanks be to God, who gives us the victory through our Lord Jesus Christ!" (1 Cor. 15:53–57).

Like the Israelites, we too forget that victory is promised us. We know more of the story than they did, yet we still turn our hearts away—forgetting that God's story is greater. But shouldn't this ultimate victory over death become our constant song, our banner of hope? Do we truly believe that Christ's victory gives us the power to walk through every life challenge?

Mom now sings her own songs of victory. She has been cancer-free for more than a decade, and now that she is retired, she volunteers much of her time checking on patients and encouraging families at the same hospital where she received treatment. Whether it's with a thoughtful email, a listening ear, a loaf of banana bread, or a tin of chocolate chip brownies, she is always ready to cheer on others with the hope that they do not fight alone.

My mom knows firsthand that there are no limits to what God can do, whether carrying someone through chemo or flooding his or her heart with His love. Confident in her identity as a child of God, she has been able to sing of victory no matter what. And, just like my aunt's cheer songs and Deborah's faith, Mom's song is contagious.

My songs of hope returned too. It took a few years of wrestling, tears, and prayers for me to finally begin to discover the victory that I had been missing during Mom's treatment. One of the passages that renewed my hope was in Paul's letter to the Philippians. The refrain that played on repeat in my mind was "I can do everything through Christ, who gives me strength" (4:13 NLT).

Paul knew beyond a shadow of a doubt that Christ had won the battle for his life by defeating death on the cross. Paul's victory had been won by Christ. Once he learned that this was true, Paul centered the rest of his life on it.

I too began to realize that one of the side effects of identity in Christ is victory—over fear, discouragement, anxiety, sin, and, in fact, all of life's storms. And what a game changer that has been. Moved by the truth that my victory came by resting in Him, I wrote a fourteen-song album about it.[5] No matter my circumstances, I was coming to accept that the battle and the outcome belong to the Lord.

Aunt Carol's fabulous cheer songs keep coming, and the mailing list has grown. And in each one, I see evidence that her joy is rooted in a deep place of peace. This peace comes from laying her worries and stresses on the One who holds her victory in His hands. Because of this, her emails, though always full of hope, are also honest. She doesn't shy away from mentioning her challenges and how she is praying through them. And she never hesitates to emphatically express her confidence in the Lord, who will carry and protect her family through every battle.

Some who have enjoyed her emails are in the thick of fighting cancer. And some, like me, have not faced that war. Others are now cancer-free, either here or in heaven. Whatever their circumstances, it turns out that a song that brings joy and strength in the Lord is a song lots of people want to hear on repeat.

Your Song of Victory

We often think victory over fear or depression comes as we live in a positive mental state. Although that is partially true, that mental state has to be rooted in a lasting truth that lives outside us—in our identity in Christ.

I encourage you to write down the words of truth that would compose your song of victory. Which specific part of God's truth, if you embraced it, would give you hope in the midst of any circumstance, no matter how dark?

You could also write a song lamenting your current lack of confidence that God will bring victory, calling on Him to guide your heart to the light of His truth. Either way, write your song to God below.

Here are some words from one of my songs to inspire your thinking as you write:

Our God, our strength, our shield,
Every time our hearts cry out, He hears.
With our song we praise Him,
Stronghold of salvation.
We lift our hands to You,
Standing on Your promise carried through,
Your arms spread wide for us,
Your daughters and Your sons,
In Christ, our inheritance.[6]

A Biblical Cheer Song

Those who belong to the Lord belong to the new kingdom of Israel, God's people. So we can memorize and sing the powerful, confident song of Deborah and Barak: *"Hear this, you kings! Listen, you rulers! I, even I, will sing to the LORD; I will praise the LORD, the God of Israel, in song"* (Judg. 5:3 NIV).

Because our hearts are prone to wander, to forget the Lord and turn to other gods, we can also sing the words He spoke through Moses: *"You will search for the LORD your God, and you will find him when you seek him with all your heart and all your soul"* (Deut. 4:29).

Hannah prayed:

My heart rejoices in the LORD; my horn is lifted up by the LORD. My mouth boasts over my enemies, because I rejoice in your salvation.

There is no one holy like the LORD. There is no one besides you! And there is no rock like our God.

Do not boast so proudly, or let arrogant words come out of your mouth, for the LORD is a God of knowledge, and actions are weighed by him.

The bows of the warriors are broken, but the feeble are clothed with strength.

Those who are full hire themselves out for food, but those who are starving hunger no more. The woman who is childless gives birth to seven, but the woman with many sons pines away.

The LORD brings death and gives life; he sends some down to Sheol, and he raises others up.

The LORD brings poverty and gives wealth; he humbles and he exalts.

He raises the poor from the dust and lifts the needy from the trash heap. He seats them with noblemen and gives them a throne of honor. For the foundations of the earth are the LORD's; he has set the world on them.

He guards the steps of his faithful ones, but the wicked perish in darkness, for a person does not prevail by his own strength.

Those who oppose the LORD will be shattered; he will thunder in the heavens against them. The LORD will judge the ends of the earth. He will give power to his king; he will lift up the horn of his anointed.

1 Samuel 2:1–10

Chapter 4

A Song of Strength

The Makeup Challenge

I was twelve when the greatest day of my life arrived. For at least a year, I had been yearning for and pleading with my mom to be allowed to wear makeup. The wait had felt like an eternity to my tween heart. So far I had only gotten to trade in my ChapStick for lip gloss. I wanted more. Despite my pleas for powders and crèmes to pile on my face, Mom's answer was always a resolute "No. You're too young."

Then one blessed day, she surrendered to my merciless begging. "You have to promise one thing," she said. "If you get makeup, you're going to put it on every day for school."

Duh, I thought. I would happily put it on two or three times a day, if I could just have some.

So off we went to the house of a friend who sold makeup for a full morning of lessons. The fun began with a light, powdery foundation suitable for a middle schooler.

Our friend patiently showed me how to get just enough on the sponge and how and where to apply it to my face. Though my blending skills were subpar, after a half hour or so of "foundationing," I sort of had it figured out. We moved on to blush. More swipes in a palette, this time with a brush, and another new motion to learn.

After another half hour of learning to swipe and blend, we were into eyeshadow and mascara. More brushes and palettes and blending techniques. More failed attempts at getting it right.

Four hours in, my face was properly made up, but my head was exploding. Makeup in real life was not nearly as much fun as the idea of makeup.

I packed up my beauty booty and headed home, exhausted. The next morning, with some trepidation, I went to the bathroom vanity and began the makeup-applying process on my own. I vaguely remembered the sponge moves for getting the foundation right. I got the blush close to where it should be. But when I got to the eyeshadow, Mom had to remind me of the steps. I was worn out before I ever left for school.

The second day was much like the first. But on the third day, I decided to skip the eyeshadow. On the fourth day, I skipped the foundation and just went for a little blush. By the fifth day, I was back to lip gloss. I informed my mother that makeup was too hard and I was giving it up.

"Oh, no you aren't," she said. "You agreed you would put it on every day. You will learn to put on makeup, because one day you will need it. And if you don't put it on, people will think it's because you're not capable. So the time to figure it out is now."

I didn't like her answer, but I knew she was right, and I'm thankful she made me stick to the process. Mom, bless her, knew that her tween daughter who loved tight-rolled jeans and dresses with massive shoulder pads—fashion forward then—and the *idea* of makeup would need these skills in a world where she'd have to fight extra hard for a place, just because she couldn't see. It was during experiences like this that I learned how to build the inner grit that would get me far in life.

Becoming blind is one of the top three fears of many people in the world. Though I didn't know that at the time, I learned early on that being different could lead to isolation and sadness unless I took matters into my own hands. Making a better life was up to me. As I practiced applying makeup—or ironing clothes, cooking, or cleaning the house—I knew all of it was preparing me for the future.

Mastering each new task gave me confidence that I could do almost anything I set my mind to and that my drive to do so would help me thrive in a sighted world. But there is a problem with this sort of inner grit. At some point, it runs out.

The work of earning and maintaining your place in the world is a relentless, endless, exhausting pursuit that eventually drains you of all your strength. Then you falter and feel like a failure. You try to recover by gritting it out, and you fail again. After a million cycles of this, I had to face the reality that inner grit was not the same as true inner strength. When I got to that point, I had to learn a new set of steps that could lead me down the path to that strength.

Nobody wants to be weak or thought of as weak. Yet we all face challenges and we all have weaknesses. How do you manage yours? Perhaps you are driven and determined like me, doing whatever it takes to always appear cool, calm, and in control. Or maybe, in total frustration, you find yourself blaming or resenting others when you feel overwhelmed by life's challenges—something I've often done as well. Or perhaps you sit in the back row and stand on the sidelines, your fear and lack of confidence whispering to you to hide from the world. I've been there too.

But what if there is another way? A way to find not only deep strength in the midst of our weakness but also deep joy. One of my teachers on strength in weakness from the Bible is Hannah, whose story and song are found at the beginning of 1 Samuel. She learned some important lessons about strength that not only changed her life but also helped change the course of history. The story of how she navigated her challenges is full of truth that can help us as we walk through our own difficulties and come to grips with our weaknesses.

Admitting Defeat

Hannah was the mother of Samuel, the great priest of Israel who eventually anointed the famous King David. But this is far from the place where she began. Hannah's story opens with the revelation of her utterly miserable circumstances. She was one of a man's two wives—and as we've already seen, that never results in peace. In fact, the other wife, Peninnah, is referred to as her "rival" (1 Sam. 1:6–7). To make matters worse, Hannah could not have children.

In today's world, being unable to conceive is an incredible heartbreak for many. But being childless in Hannah's day meant that a woman had no value whatsoever. Society had absolutely no sympathy for someone suffering in this way.[1]

Year after year, Hannah, Peninnah, and their husband, Elkanah, traveled to the tabernacle in Shiloh to worship God (v. 3). And year after year, Peninnah would bully Hannah because she had no children. Every year, "Hannah would weep and would not eat" (v. 7). Hannah's loving but super-insensitive husband would ask her why she was crying: "Am I not better to you than ten sons?" (v. 8).

Though we don't have insight into Hannah's life beyond the tabernacle, we do know that Elkanah loved her very much (v. 5), and we can infer that she was likely Elkanah's first wife. Not only is she named first (v. 2), but he probably would not have taken a second wife if the first one had been able to conceive. We can imagine, then, that Hannah didn't spend every day grieving.

I bet she often tapped into her own inner grit—going about her day-to-day, responding to her husband's love, and maintaining calm around Peninnah and her kids. Yet because of her infertility, Hannah lived in a perpetual state of sadness and longing. For her, all the pain and drama came to a head every year at the time of worship. She was a true victim—battling infertility, lack of empathy from her husband, and bullying from the other wife.

Then came the moment at Shiloh when Hannah had had enough. Broken and defeated, she chose to step away from the chaos that had previously always distracted her from worshipping the Lord, reducing her instead to tears and the inability to eat anything (v. 7). She ran straight into the arms of Yahweh, laying before Him all the things that had so far held them miles apart. He met her there in her brokenness. It was in this meeting with God, this place of emptying and receiving, that Hannah found true strength.

For most of my life, the mental noise of navigating a sighted world without sight has kept me from trusting completely that God actually wants to give me relentless strength. Ever since I can remember, my tendency has been to rely on my own abilities instead of leaning on Him with my full weight.

About the same time that I began to experience the joy of makeup, I felt the pain of bullying. In middle school, kids were cruel. Some of it was run-of-the-mill adolescent behavior: whispers and giggles because of my new haircut or the wrong answer I gave when called on by a teacher. But being the only blind student at the public school where I spent half my day meant I also experienced the full force of some unique bullying.

Someone would steal my lunch in the cafeteria, and everyone at the table would laugh. Kids would complain loudly enough for all to hear when it was their turn to guide me through an unfamiliar area. I got called *stupid* a lot. I also got to spend lots of days alone on the playground. The abuse left me feeling weak, insignificant, and alone.

After one of the darkest days of bullying, my mom gently told me, "Ginny, Jesus is always your best friend. But some days it may feel like He's your only friend." She assured me I could tell Him everything, because not only did He see and know everything I was facing, but He had also experienced the worst bullying and the worst darkness imaginable. To cry out to Him was to cry out to a God who knew my struggles firsthand.

I accepted her words in theory, but I didn't know how to tap into the strength He could give. I thought that even though He was there to hear prayers and oversee things, my inner strength was the key to my success. It has taken me years to learn that possessing unwavering, true inner strength involves being vulnerable and meeting with God again and again.

Meeting with God

Hannah is a beautiful example of meeting with God in vulnerability. She entered the tabernacle, and in deep brokenness with many tears, she poured out her heart to the Lord (1 Sam. 1:10). She did not resign herself to her circumstances and just praise anyway. She brought her aching heart and passionately prayed about the thing that weighed her down the most.

In her weakness, she went to the Lord and offered up her desire to the only One who could bring change: "LORD of Armies, if you will take notice of your servant's affliction, remember and not forget me, and give your servant a son, I will give him to the LORD all the days of his life" (v. 11).

Several things are immediately clear in Hannah's prayer. Hannah knew that the Lord she was talking to is all powerful—she called Him "LORD of Armies" (or "LORD of hosts" ESV). She was directing her prayer to the One who held her life—and the world—in His capable hands. Because she knew these things about the Lord, she knew her prayer was not falling on deaf ears.

Hannah's longing for children then came to the surface, revealing another beautiful, powerful aspect of prayer. Because the God of creation cares about every detail of our lives, meeting Him in prayer requires our total honesty and total trust that He hears and wants to work in every longing we lay before Him.

We learn more about how to pray from Hannah's conversation with Eli, the priest. In this dark time in Israel, Eli wasn't used to seeing people pour out their hearts to God, and he mistakenly accused Hannah of being drunk (v. 14). Hannah insisted she was sober. She was simply "a woman with a broken heart ... praying from the depth of [her] anguish and resentment" (vv. 15–16).

Hannah didn't pray for only a son. She also gave God the anxiety and bitterness that had been holding her prisoner. Hannah laid on the Lord her deepest longings, her deepest sadness, and her deepest darkness. She gave all that was in the recesses of her heart to the God who created her.

And now no walls stood between them. In the confessing, the lamenting, and the offering of Hannah's prayer, we see God's empowering begin. Hannah vulnerably voiced her total weakness to Eli, and her honesty and humility provoked him to offer her a blessing (v. 17).

Hannah got up from her place of prayer a changed woman. Though she didn't know what the Lord's answer would be, she walked away from the encounter finally able to eat. Her face was different too—she no longer wore the expression of a weak, hopeless woman (v. 18). She had laid her cares on the shoulders of the One who could carry them best. She had offered God her weakness, and He had stabilized her with His strength. She had given God her desire, and He had given her Himself. Now she could go and worship Him in hope, regardless of what would happen next (v. 19).

At our core, many of us believe that while prayer is a nice idea, it is actually up to us to save ourselves. I have lots of friends who rely on the relentless inner grit they've developed. Their relationship with God is distant—respectful perhaps—but they aren't interested in meeting with Him.

And there's a reason. Day in and day out, they have battled specific life challenges. They've cried out to God in the past, but no answer arrived. No miracle took place. So they assume that if there's a God, He must not care about our daily challenges. Or perhaps He wants us to figure things out on our own. Or maybe He isn't actually good.

It can be painful to think of a caring, loving, listening God when our circumstances are so overwhelming. So instead of going to God with all our deepest resentment, anger, sadness, and desires, we trust in our own strength. We perfect the art of our makeup, as it were, and face the world all on our own.

This is certainly where I used to live. I didn't talk to God much about people's reactions to my blindness. I assumed it was a trial meant to toughen me up. I figured that if I ever became a super-Christian, I'd be able to rise above it all. I'm thankful to be long past the bullying era, but the fear and misunderstanding I'm often met with—and the accompanying feeling that I am less than—have sometimes left me brokenhearted. At times I've chosen to feel like a victim.

I was explaining this to a friend one day.

"I have done everything I can to prove myself," I lamented. "I run my own business, and I've had great adventures as a musician. And I think I'm generally well put together. So why can't I meet people's expectations? Why am I often seen as someone to be pitied instead of an equal—or a potential friend?" After thinking for a moment, I admitted perhaps the more honest question: "Why can't I meet my own expectations?"

My friend happens to be an avid prayer warrior and a life coach. "What do you think God thinks of your struggles?" she asked. "How do you think He feels when He sees people being unkind or dismissive? Or when He sees the unbelievable pressure you put on yourself?"

I did not know.

As I prayed and asked God to show me, He began to reveal His heart. Jesus healed people with all types of challenges, inviting others out of their fear and doubt, and weeping before He raised Lazarus from the dead—the stories leapt out at me from the pages of the Bible in a way they never had before. I realized how He aches because of the suffering in the world and the sadness I (and the rest of us) feel.

His longing was for me to come to Him, to be honest and vulnerable, and to empty everything in the recesses of my heart as Hannah did. I hadn't taken to Him my sadness and frustration over the challenges of being blind, and I had held many other things back as well. Trying to manage in my own strength had driven a wedge between us.

As I read His words and met Him in prayer, seeing and experiencing the beauty of His heart, His strength took root in me, overpowering my weak, human version of strength. And I began to change. Though my circumstances were not different, as with Hannah, my heart started to rise above them in a chorus of true strength.

Strength in Weakness

Hannah's next prayer (1 Sam. 2:1–10) shows us that true strength is not found inside ourselves. It grows as we pour our hearts out to a holy God, inviting Him into the midst of our anguish and our longings, where He most teaches us to trust and love Him.

Hannah sang of how she became wrapped in the joy and strength of the Lord instead of in her own circumstances. In her song, we hear that true strength—strength to face our darkest days and rise above our enemies—comes when we rest our overworked and exhausted souls in the arms of the only One who can renew our strength. As we learn to lean on Him, our love for Him grows, as does a deep joy we can't find anywhere else.

To borrow a quote from a Benedictine monk, "Joy is the happiness that doesn't depend on what happens."[2] It is the inner smile that remains through trials. As we will see, by the time Hannah sang her song, she had already both received a son and given him back to the Lord (1:27–28). Yet her joy was intact. Her song is not about her son but about her Lord, her rock, who gave her strength (2:1–2).

In Hannah's song of strength, she sang about her great God who reverses fortunes—giving children to the childless woman and filling the hungry (v. 5). Her all-powerful God brings poverty, but He also lifts up the poor, granting them "a throne of honor" (vv. 7–8). Hannah also sang of failure for those who trust their own strength instead of God's strength (vv. 3, 9). She had learned these things firsthand. God allowed her to be childless for some time (1:5–7), and then He gave her—a weary, heckled, misunderstood, childless woman—a son (v. 20).

After raising her son for several years, Hannah willingly gave him back to God, as she had promised, taking him to the tabernacle to live with the Lord. "I prayed for this boy," she said, "and since the LORD gave me what I asked him for, I now give the boy to the LORD" (vv. 20–28). We don't have a category for this type of action today, but one of my seminary professors had a helpful analogy. He said it would be sort of like sending your child to boarding school and visiting him only once or twice a year.

When Hannah went to worship at the tabernacle year after year, she brought her son new clothes she had made for him (2:19). How astounding is that? Hannah returned to the place of worship with her husband and her rival, and like before, she did so with no child. But now Hannah was different. Now she sang. She worshipped.

Every year, Eli would bless Hannah and her husband, asking God to give them more children, and He did … but not immediately (vv. 19–21). How could Hannah sing and worship in these circumstances—essentially childless? Quite simply, Hannah's Lord, not her longing, was now at the center of her soul.

Hannah's meeting with God brought her to a faith that was at once childlike and mature. She now believed that God was in charge and that loving Him above all else gave her strength to do even the most difficult things. In other words, Hannah's strength came from trusting God's strength. From trusting that He was in control of her life and of what happens in the world. As she looked to Him for her identity and rested in Him, her song of true strength emerged.

I've written a chorus that says it this way:

> *Thank You, Lord.*
> *You don't always give me what I ask for.*
> *Even when I'm crying out that I'm sure,*
> *You see what I can't see and give me what I need.*[3]

The reason I struggle daily to live in God's strength is that it means I have to be okay with being weak. Though you might think blindness is my greatest obstacle, my internal weaknesses are much more challenging. The great weakness for a driven "entertainer" like me is worrying about how I am perceived. Yet as I rest in my identity in Christ, I find true strength. I know that my grit—that drive and determination—will never be enough to sustain me, nor will the attitudes of others be enough to break me. With the love of the God of creation surrounding me, how can I not release to Him my need to control what other people think of me?

How does this play out in real life? It means I try to look at myself the way the Lord sees me—as His dearly loved daughter, the recipient of Christ's finished work on the cross. I don't look at how I or anyone else evaluates me. As Timothy Keller has said, "The essence of Gospel humility is not thinking more of myself or less of myself, it is thinking of myself less."[4]

If others think I'm weak, that's fine. They're right—I can't do life on my own, and I'm becoming ever more confident in that fact. Resting in God's strength means I don't focus on making myself look impressive or insisting on my independence. It means I sometimes accept help I don't need, just to have the opportunity to connect with someone new. It means I can focus my attention on doing what He has put in front of me: serving, encouraging, helping bring change, and being unafraid to be vulnerable. It means my inner grit now comes from the power of the cross.

I realized at some point that my drive to appear strong had put a wall not only between God and me but also between me and others. Turns out, people have lots of questions about how I do life, and my lack of vulnerability had kept them from asking. Now I have a video series called *How I See It*, where I show how I accomplish everyday tasks like putting on makeup.

And once again, as I've seen with my songs, when I open up and share, others begin to share their own vulnerabilities and questions. Being honest has invited others into honesty as well, revealing that none of us can do life in our own strength.

The Bigger Story

Only God could work through Hannah's suffering to bring hope to us. Little did she know that her son would lead Israel out of the darkest period they had ever known. Little did she know that young Samuel would find resilient strength in the Lord as his mother had or that he would challenge the nation of Israel to once again find its strength in God.

Hannah also confidently sang of things that hadn't happened yet. She sang of the anointed one to come, not knowing that Israel would soon be led by anointed kings instead of judges. Not knowing that this son of hers would go on to anoint King David, the king after God's own heart.

Nor could she know that, a thousand years later, another joyful song of strength would be sung by a young woman soon to deliver God's ultimate anointed King:

> He has done a mighty deed with his arm;
> he has scattered the proud
> because of the thoughts of their hearts....
> He has helped his servant Israel,
> remembering his mercy
> to Abraham and his descendants forever.
>   (Luke 1:51, 54–55)

Both Hannah and Mary sang of how weak and powerless humans are and how strong and powerful God is. What's more, they sang of how He loves and remembers His people. In His love, God chose to become weak so that we could gain eternal strength. "He was oppressed and afflicted, yet he did not open his mouth. Like a lamb led to the slaughter and like a sheep silent before her shearers, he did not open his mouth" (Isa. 53:7).

The more we are moved by Jesus' choice to empty Himself and become weak on our behalf, the more wholeheartedly we can sing of—and live in—the strength He gives.

Your Song of Strength

I like to think of our lives as songs being written. Every moment, we are singing words and melodies to the world around us—and not just in the moments we think are important. If that's true, wouldn't it be great to sing hopeful songs? Songs that declare our own weakness and the joy of the One who gives lasting strength?

I love how Paul, the boldest and seemingly strongest of people, spoke about weakness. He had a specific weakness—"a thorn in the flesh," as he called it—that constantly plagued him. "Concerning this," he wrote, "I pleaded with the Lord three times that it would leave me. But he said to me, 'My grace is sufficient for you, for my power is perfected in weakness.' Therefore, I will most gladly boast all the more about my weaknesses, so that Christ's power may reside in me" (2 Cor. 12:7–10). The original Greek paints a picture of Christ's power being a tabernacle over him. The more Paul embraced the reality that he couldn't do it on his own, the more Christ's strength enfolded him.

I have to admit, I don't always want to sing a song like this. I'd rather sing about my own strength. But the Lord says that a more beautiful song is the one all about how He works in our weakness.

I invite you to bring your song of brokenness, tears, pain, questions—whatever you need to give to God—and write it in this space.

Remember that He loves lifting up the poor in spirit and giving strength to the weak. Or if you have a deep sense of His joy, then, by all means, sing about that! Whatever your song is today, here are some words from my heart's song to inspire you:

> *You were made for more than breathin'—*
> *More than playin' small and runnin' scared.*
> *You were made to walk in freedom—*
> *To love and laugh, to find out why you're here.*
> *Your name was known before the earth was formed.*
> *You were made for more.*[5]

God's Song of Strength

Hannah sang of who God is. As truth took root in her life, her strength grew. Let's learn these words from her song today: *"There is no one holy like the LORD. There is no one besides you! And there is no rock like our God" (1 Sam. 2:2).*

Let's also memorize the words that Jesus said to Paul—can you imagine how many times he sang these words during his challenging life? *"He said to me, 'My grace is sufficient for you, for my power is perfected in weakness'" (2 Cor. 12:9).*

The LORD is my shepherd; I shall not want.

He makes me lie down in green pastures. He leads me beside still waters.

He restores my soul. He leads me in paths of righteousness for his name's sake.

Even though I walk through the valley of the shadow of death, I will fear no evil, for you are with me; your rod and your staff, they comfort me.

You prepare a table before me in the presence of my enemies; you anoint my head with oil; my cup overflows.

Surely goodness and mercy shall follow me all the days of my life, and I shall dwell in the house of the LORD forever.

Psalm 23 ESV

Chapter 5

A Song of Rest

Disquiet in the Quiet

It's a lovely spring morning in 2020 as I sit writing in the living room of my four-hundred-square-foot New York City apartment. In the couple of years I've been here, the noise of the bustling city drifting in through my front window has become a familiar and comfortable companion.

But today the street outside my window is eerily quiet—as it has been every day for the past month. Only the ambulances break the silence, sounding their sirens at least once every half hour.

Each day, the death toll rises. And so does the anxiety of uncertainty.

Who would have thought the world could so quickly descend into such deep darkness? But here we are.

We're learning what it means to experience the unknown. We're learning about suffering too incredible to wrap our minds around. And we're learning how to adapt to a strange new way of living— secluded in our homes with family members or roommates or, as in my case, endlessly alone. As the drama drags on, we try to navigate the new rhythms of uneasiness beating in our hearts.

As I write this, I've had mild COVID-19 symptoms for ten days now—low-grade fever, aches, shortness of breath, total exhaustion.

I'm not sick enough to be tested, but friends in the medical profession think I probably have the virus. I'm thankful the symptoms aren't worse, but I'm ready to feel like myself again. Since I've been forced into this slower pace, I've been thinking a lot.

I think about the health care workers on the front lines of the battle, and I pray that they would be protected and have hopeful hearts. I pray for those who are isolated, especially those with disabilities and those in the twilight of life. I pray for those who were instantly unemployed or who have lost their businesses. On some level, I feel their pain: all my concerts for the foreseeable future have been canceled.

I wonder what we'll learn from this season. What we'll say when we look back. On the other side of all this, what will we be like as a world? I wonder if there are words that could bring peace in the midst of a pandemic—and if those words are somehow in me.

I ruminate on words that have brought me immense comfort in the past to see if they still do: "The LORD is my shepherd; I lack nothing. He makes me lie down in green pastures. He leads me beside still waters. He restores my soul" (Ps. 23:1–3 NHEB).

I was seven or eight when Mom taught the Twenty-Third Psalm to me and my brother, JD. Though I was exceedingly proud to have memorized it, I wasn't sure what it meant. I think it was the language of the King James Version that brought on the mystery for this southern kid. Did "I shall not want" mean I wasn't allowed to want anything? And I loathed the idea of being *made* to lie down anywhere.

Now, as a grown-up, I understand what this psalm means in theory, though I still resist its call. Perhaps you are the same. We love the idea of the Lord being our shepherd, guiding us—especially through seasons of uncertainty. We love the idea of peace in any place—even in the presence of our enemies or on our darkest days. But for most of us, finding that peace is rare, if it happens at all.

Why is peace so elusive? Why is anxiety so much easier to come by than the rest God promises us?

How do we experience the feeling of calm that David sang about here?

In the course of time, the lyrics of this song have become deeply rooted in my soul. Through seasons of heartache and change, they have whispered tenderly to me of a God who is not just a great Creator but a loving Shepherd who is caring for, protecting, and guiding us through every moment. In recent years I've returned to it often to meditate, its words singing deeper comfort to me now than ever before. Let's open it together to find the rest David sang of so we can sing of it too.

True Rest in Chaos

Christianity is the only faith that insists there is a Rest-Giver who holds us in the midst of chaos. No other major religion has such a notion. In our secular culture, where we say the key to having hope and peace lies within *us*, we are especially full of fear these days. How can we possibly comfort ourselves when our world has been turned upside down and we clearly have no control?

Popular voices in our current cultural space have their own recommendations: detach and toughen up (Stoicism), embrace suffering with grace (Buddhism), or accept that suffering has come because of the sins of our past lives (karma).

One of my favorite life-hack podcasters recently interviewed a Buddhist monk and multiple proponents of Stoic philosophy, concluding that we can cultivate inner rest and the power to accept our circumstances.[1] But if Christianity is true, we can accept our circumstances not with resignation but with hope, knowing we have Someone to go to with our wailing and our worry. Someone who, whether He gives us immediate answers or not, will give us lasting hope in the midst of our darkness.

The Lord Jesus uniquely said, "Come to me, all of you who are weary and burdened, and I will give you rest" (Matt. 11:28). Christianity is the only faith in which God provides for, protects, and guides His children—and carries their troubles in every season. And just as important, He gives purpose to the chaos in which we find ourselves.

Billy Graham once said, "Mountaintops are for views and inspiration, but fruit is grown in the valleys."[2] I agree. It would be impossible to fully appreciate the joy of light if we didn't know what darkness felt like. We wouldn't be able to bask in its radiance if we hadn't first lived without it. But if there were no Shepherd leading us, what purpose would darkness have? What could we emerge with on the other side, other than grit or bitterness?

The psalmists, including David, experienced their fair share of suffering. So when they sang of God's peace and rest, it was in the context of a world where they faced danger, plague, famine, and fatality. But they reached for God in their chaos again and again, leaning on Him for comfort and protection.

As a shepherd who battled lions and bears, who fought for his life many times, David knew what it was to be overwhelmed with fear. But he had also come to know deep rest, and he sang of it in this psalm and many others.

Before we dive in to see what David can teach us about knowing God as our shepherd and friend, a quick word. David and other psalmists and prophets, not to mention Job, took before the Lord their laments and complaints about what befell them. Our Shepherd can handle our anger, sorrow, and questions about deep suffering. We will return to a song of lament in a later chapter, but for now, let's discover how David experienced true rest in the care of the Lord, his Shepherd.

Contentment, Rest, and Freedom

In the first section of Psalm 23, we hear only of the actions the Shepherd takes for His sheep. David's contented response was to want for nothing (v. 1). The Shepherd made him lie down in peaceful places, led him by quiet waters, and restored him (vv. 2–3). The Shepherd has provided everything we need: rest, quiet, and protection, renewing our minds and our souls with Himself and His truth. Derek Kidner helpfully said, "The shepherd lives with his flock and is everything to it: guide, physician and protector."[3]

To rest in the care of our Shepherd is an active pursuit. Just as we would seek the wisdom of the people who love and protect us, we listen actively to what God has to say. We tune our hearts to His promises. We fill our minds with His words of comfort and peace. We remember all the ways He has been faithful to us in the past. We cry out to Him with our concerns and ask for His help. As we do, our hearts naturally open to receive His rest.

The Lord our Shepherd always leads His sheep in the right path because it brings glory to His name. As David said in Psalm 119:32, "I run in the path of your commandments, for you have set my heart free" (NHEB). Our Shepherd never says, "Go figure out the right road—the one that will lead you to the best place for you, little sheep." Instead, He says, "I, your loving shepherd, delight in nothing more than leading you down the right and best road—the path of life" (see Isa. 24:17). As we walk down this path, we find a better kind of freedom than we could ever find on our own.

For most of us, the idea of "God's right path" leads us to think of living pious, disciplined lives—the connotation being *legalism*. Some of us rail against the idea that we should behave in a certain way to please God. Others see it as a bargaining tool—if we follow Him to the best of our ability, God will give us what we want, including His peace. But following God's right path is so much better than mere obedience or getting what we want. It is designed with our best in mind, leading us to the life, hope, and peace He wants to give us.

Instruments like pianos and guitars must be tuned to some standard outside the instrument (like a tuning fork or an app). Otherwise, they could not play together and be in tune. In the same way, true freedom comes for us as our actions are tuned to God's perfect pitch.

God wants us to follow His path so that we may love Him more, love one another better, and also love ourselves healthily—so we grow in wisdom, strength, and even joy on our way to being together with Him forever. When we follow our own path, we can see only what we're doing in the moment—not how what we're doing affects others or even ourselves long-term. Because we don't know the lasting impact of our choices, the best idea is to trust the One who does, following His road to inner freedom and unending peace.

How to Fight Fear

The psalmist went on to sing about when God's right path for him leads through the valley of the shadow of death (Ps. 23:4). This valley is a steep-sided Middle Eastern ravine, where the walls are high enough that the sheep can't see the sun. They would be afraid as they walked through it.

But even when the "right path" for the Lord's sheep leads through the dark valley, we need not be afraid. Why? Because the Shepherd—who has met all our needs, has given us His protection so we can rest, and clearly sees the right path ahead—is going every step of the way with us, even through the deepest shadow. His rod and staff, the tools that protect and guide His sheep on the right path, also give us comfort along the way (v. 4).

Interestingly, it's a question not of *if* but of *when* this would be David's path. David could have been talking about actual death here, but he was more likely talking about a season that feels dark and scary—like death. Either way, he knew that this shadowed path was inevitable. But he would not fear harm, because the Shepherd was with him.

This brings to mind the prophet Isaiah's words from God to His beloved people—a people who had gone so far off the right path that now He had to lead them through the darkest valley. He would protect them, but they still had to go through it.

> I will be with you when you pass through the
>   waters,
> and when you pass through the rivers,
> they will not overwhelm you.

You will not be scorched
when you walk through the fire,
and the flame will not burn you.
For I [am] Yahweh your God,
the Holy One of Israel, and your Savior.
(Isa. 43:2–3 HCSB)

What is interesting here is what the Lord, the Shepherd-King, did *not* say. He did not say, "Do not fear, for I will fix it." He said, "Do not fear, for I am your God." In other words, "No matter the circumstance, I am all you need." In Psalm 23, David declared his trust: he would not be afraid in the difficult valley, because the One who holds all things was holding him.

Thinking on these words reminds me of a long, scary season I went through several years ago. It began while on tour at Christmas, when I started to lose my ability to sing higher notes. After listening to me work through a host of exercises, a vocal specialist told me I might never be able to fully recover my voice. Despite her prognosis, I started doing vocal therapies with a coach in hopes that things would change.

Bit by bit, I made progress, but singing was difficult for the next year. As I continued to do concerts, I realized that not only were my vocal cords hurting but my abdomen was too. Several visits to the doctor and multiple scans later, I was headed into emergency surgery to remove a tumor, with the possibility of cancer. I wouldn't know the results until I woke up.

I can still feel the knot in the pit of my stomach when I think about that time. But there were several ways God spoke to me of His love in the middle of it all. My longtime friends from college—Sylvia, Charlynn, and Dea—not only called often to check in and chat but also happily agreed to celebrate my birthday at a non-exciting, health-food restaurant, as eating well made me feel somehow better about the whole thing. My friend Cindy called often to listen to and pray with me.

Talking to God and being with friends who reflected Him so beautifully reminded me that He is faithful and good and that He would be with me regardless of what I found out. Meditating on these truths calmed my anxious heart. I knew He might not deliver me from the threat of cancer or from my messed-up vocal cords. And even though I wasn't eager to face either of those challenges long-term, I had experienced enough of His care and His rest to know He would guide me through.

Thankfully my voice is now stronger than ever, the surgery was a success, and I didn't have cancer. Yet I will never forget that season and how I experienced firsthand that I am not in charge of my destiny. I will never forget how God helped me see that He is holding me close in every moment—even the most excruciating ones.

Our Shepherd, King, and Friend

After singing about the valley of the shadow of death, David sang of his Shepherd as a generous, hospitable king—but a king who knew him intimately.

In the ancient Near East, *shepherd* was a common metaphor for a king. So in Psalm 23:1–4 and 6, David was meditating on the Lord as a shepherd—protecting him and caring for all his needs—and in verse 5, he reflected on Him as a king who intimately knew him and cared for him as a friend. The Lord was the preparer of a feast that David would enjoy in the presence of his enemies. This king and friend tended to David's needs, rejuvenating him by cleansing his head with oil. As a result, David's heart was full (v. 5).

This image conjures a vivid picture in my mind. Though I don't have literal enemies that I'm aware of, I'm reminded of the times in school when I felt surrounded by bullies. Or the times in my adult life when I have been surrounded by people whose misconceptions about me felt insurmountable. In challenging times, David said, we are not alone. The Lord is tending to our needs. Caring for us. Longing to sit and talk with us, no matter what enemy surrounds us. Even if it's a pandemic. Or cancer. Or unkind people. Or anxiety and fear. He "has a celebration meal with us not after we finally get out of the dark valley but in the middle of it, in the presence of our enemies. He wants us to rejoice in him in the midst of our troubles."[4]

This verse is not merely the stuff of kitschy artwork. Picture the scene: The Lord has an intimate feast with you, but it's not in an idyllic atmosphere. He talks to you of His love and His promises and tenderly refreshes you as you feel attacked from all sides.

How do we find peace in this place?

We pursue God, knowing that He is always pursuing us.

We will be incapable of finding joy and strength in our suffering unless we make a constant practice of crying out to God. If He is our shepherd-protector, royal provider, and close friend, why would we not tell Him all that weighs on us and ask for what we need? It is through dialoguing with God in prayer and listening to His words in Scripture that we are able to be confident that His love surrounds us, even in the moments when we can't feel it.

The more we do this, the more quickly our hearts will settle into a place of peace. And the more easily we will be able to sing joyfully with the psalmist, "LORD, you are my portion and my cup of blessing; you hold my future" (Ps. 16:5).

Surrounded

Now we get to the section of the Twenty-Third Psalm that has more recently made my heart explode with awe and delight every time I think about it. The Lord the shepherd is leading. But His goodness and love are following, pursuing us in every moment (v. 6). As one commentator has said, "Goodness and love act like the shepherd's sheepdogs, helping the shepherd to keep the sheep going in the right direction."[5]

I love dogs. In college I had a yellow Labrador guide dog named Lindy. More recently I've had Bailey and Lewie, both mini Australian shepherds. Bailey was twelve pounds, Lewie is thirty, and Lindy the Lab was ninety. But all of them have seen it as their job to follow me everywhere, supervise my every move, and make sure I head in the right direction. And even when I've insisted otherwise, they've herded me wherever they thought I should be going—to bed or to the kitchen for their treats or in the direction of the tree where the squirrels live. They also have protected me fiercely from every passing creature, whether friend or foe.

How much more beautiful, wonderful, and powerful are God's goodness and loving-kindness in pursuit of us! The Lord makes sure we are surrounded by them.

The Bigger Story

The Shepherd provides for us, so we lack nothing. He guides us into rest. With His rod and staff, He takes us on the right paths, leading us to life. In our deep darkness, He is with us. When the world seems like it can't get any worse, He takes the time to prepare a feast for us, talk intimately with us, rinse off our grime, and cool our heads. And His goodness and mercy are always at our heels.

In the climactic ending of the song, David celebrated the fact that he would dwell in the Lord's house for all his days! Where else would he want to be other than living and luxuriating in the presence of his shepherd, friend, and king? Where would *we* want to be other than in His presence, now and forever?

Today we have an even greater hope than David had. God sent Jesus to us as the shepherd in the flesh. He comes running when one of us is missing (Luke 15:4–7). He is the Shepherd who knows our names and whose voice we hear and know (John 10:3–4). The Shepherd who went through the darkest valley of death, laying down His life for His sheep, so we could live with Him forever (v. 11). We don't go to His temple, but we find Him in the temple of our hearts until the day we are united face to face. Until then, He guides us on the path to Himself, teaching us to love Him and sacrifice for one another, just as He has done for us (1 John 3:16).

Your Song of Rest

The key to finding rest—to believing that our Shepherd is enough for us in every season—is to sing that truth to ourselves over and over again. As we do, we are able to receive the trust and rest given us more easily.

Today, write your song of rest. Perhaps it is a song in which you thank your shepherd, king, and friend for all the ways He has cared for you this week. Maybe you want to sing of all His great attributes—His goodness, His power, His ability to see everything ... all the reasons for why you know you can trust Him. Or perhaps your song today is a prayer asking that you would sense His shepherd's love and care for you.

Here are some words from one of my favorite hymns to inspire your thinking:

> *Be still, my soul: the Lord is on your side.*
> *Bear patiently the cross of grief or pain.*
> *Leave to your God to order and provide;*
> *In every change, He faithful will remain.*
> *Be still, my soul: your best, your heav'nly Friend*
> *Through thorny ways leads to a joyful end.*[6]

God's Song of Rest

Today let's memorize all of Psalm 23. To help you, feel free to choose a translation you're familiar with. Here is one I like:

> The LORD is my shepherd; I have what I need. He lets me lie down in green pastures; he leads me beside quiet waters. He renews my life; he leads me along the right paths for his name's sake. Even when I go through the darkest valley, I fear no danger, for you are with me; your rod and your staff—they comfort me. You prepare a table before me in the presence of my enemies; you anoint my head with oil; my cup overflows. Only goodness and faithful love will pursue me all the days of my life, and I will dwell in the house of the LORD as long as I live. (CSB)

Be gracious to me, God, according to your faithful love; according to your abundant compassion, blot out my rebellion.

Completely wash away my guilt and cleanse me from my sin.

For I am conscious of my rebellion, and my sin is always before me.

Against you—you alone—I have sinned and done this evil in your sight. So you are right when you pass sentence; you are blameless when you judge....

Surely you desire integrity in the inner self, and you teach me wisdom deep within....

Turn your face away from my sins and blot out all my guilt.

God, create a clean heart for me and renew a steadfast spirit within me.

Do not banish me from your presence or take your Holy Spirit from me.

Restore the joy of your salvation to me, and sustain me by giving me a willing spirit.

Then I will teach the rebellious your ways, and sinners will return to you....

Lord, open my lips, and my mouth will declare your praise....

The sacrifice pleasing to God is a broken spirit. You will not despise a broken and humbled heart, God.

Psalm 51:1–4, 6, 9–13, 15, 17

Chapter 6

A Lament for the Misoriented Life

The Inside Truth

Being raised a good southern girl has its upsides. My DNA dictates pervasive politeness and a genuine interest in what others are up to. I can chat about the superficial—how the weather is today, how it was yesterday, which are the best restaurants in the area—for an impressive amount of time. And though my personal style is to be understated, I do not go out unless I am put together. Being finished on the outside is the key to my inner confidence. Goal number one is presenting well so others can see that I am independent and competent.

To complement my put-together exterior, I, as a southern-born blind girl, have learned that the most important vibe to give off is that I'm okay. That I'm as put together, as pristine, and as positive on the inside as I am on the outside. To mention that I am not okay would not be okay. To mention that I am dark on the inside would make people squirm.

My gut says it isn't just me who aims to present well and is slow to come forth with the truth. What about you? Do you aim to always be okay? Do you feel the weight of your darkness—mean thoughts, unmentionable desires, things you've done that you pray no one discovers? Do you keep trying to do things differently and keep tripping up? We watch as we cross lines we swore we'd never cross—or would never cross again. We hear ourselves saying things we regret even as they flow out of our mouths. We wonder what came over us.

Why do we do these things? And how do we stop?

I believe King David has some answers for us. During one of his darkest seasons, a time when he had essentially wronged everyone he knew and turned wholeheartedly from God, he was awakened by the words of a close friend who spoke God's truth to him. As we consider his story, we will discover why our hope and power lie in lamenting before the Lord about our misoriented lives.

I will also share with you my own story of turning away from God—and how I returned to Him to discover true freedom and restoration.

Why Must We Talk about Sin?

The Bible is full of prayers and stories about human depravity and failure, but many of us avoid these passages in our personal study. And we rarely hear them at church. Instead, we set our focus on the Lord's love and grace. We have good reason: Grace is the most beautiful and encouraging news! Also, we know what damage churches have done by hyperfocusing on sin. The church has long been infamous for its legalism and judgment instead of its generosity and love. And many have deep wounds because of the damage done.

But here's something I've learned: unless we know how desperately off the path we are, grace means little more than a fleeting, "warm hug" feeling. When we catch a vision of how much self-imposed darkness we've been rescued from, grace explodes our hearts with joy and deep gratitude because God has given us Himself and set us free from our chains of sin.

So in this chapter we will find our way to costly grace and sweet freedom. But first I need to walk us through the darkness of sin to get there.

There is darkness in every human heart. Even those who are not convinced of God's existence know this from personal experience. We spend our lives trying to manage the darkness inside through perfecting habits like self-discipline, constructive thinking, and positive self-talk. No doubt all these traits help us navigate and thrive in life. But for any of us who have been relentlessly trying to bring our wills into submission this way, we know how often we fall off the wagon. We lose our tempers. We have many moments of weakness and do things we regret.

We can see we will never make it to perfection at the rate we're going.

The shame we feel for not being self-disciplined enough weighs on us—often even more than sin itself. We need someone outside ourselves, not only to supernaturally conquer our self-imposed darkness of heart but also to lift the burden of it and carry away our guilt and shame once and for all.

This is why King David has much to teach us about singing to God of the nightmare our sin has brought about—until He restores us, empowering us to sing of true joy and worship again.

Psalm 51, as Derek Kidner helpfully offered, "comes from David's blackest moment of self-knowledge, yet it explores not only the depths of his guilt but some of the farthest reaches of salvation."[1]

Several of King David's sins made it into his story, but the most well-known are his affair with Bathsheba, a married woman, and his subsequent ordering of her husband Uriah's murder. After Uriah had been killed, David married his widow. In 2 Samuel 11, David— the humble shepherd, the wise king, and the author and singer of many of our favorite songs of hope—found himself drowning in sin before he knew what was happening. He covered it all up at first, but then Nathan, God's prophet—aka David's accountability partner—called him out. Once his sin was exposed, David grieved over it before the Lord, and he found his hope restored.

David's actions had many consequences, not least of which is that we're still talking about his sin three thousand years later. But the consequence of his song of repentance is that we learn how to run from our sin, guilt, and shame into the arms of One who can drive them as far as the east is from the west and restore us to wholeness.

The Hazy Season

I remember a season in which the need for such a song became more real to me than ever.

When I say I lived in a haze for a season, I mean my (figurative) vision was never clear. My mental calculator was off. My wisdom had gone missing. Everything was everyone else's fault. I was afraid of things I should have been thankful for and unmotivated to take advantage of great opportunities. God seemed nowhere to be found.

And church, I was certain, was not the place to find Him. It was full of hypocrites.

There might have been a modicum of truth in these feelings, but it was just enough to be twisted into lies I delighted in nursing.

I remember how my life unraveled before me in that season, again and again, until I felt helpless, anxious, and desperately alone. I remember the endless nights of lying on the floor with many tears. I remember how the glass of wine I occasionally enjoyed turned into several glasses of wine I needed to cope with the darkness.

The tears eventually began to flow less frequently, and the nights became less traumatic, but the perpetual haze I wandered around in lingered long.

What I remember most about that time was that I brought the darkness entirely on myself. My failure—my sin—temporarily wrecked my happiness and my peace. Thanks to me, my song of hope was replaced with a disgruntled, deflated song.

I didn't just wake up one day and make a huge, dumb decision. No, I took one small step after another in a dumb direction until I was in over my head. Until life felt out of control and I couldn't find my way back to the right path.

Even now, all these years later, I cringe at the helpless feeling I get just writing about this. I live in a place of hope and true freedom now, but the consequences of my actions still reverberate. I regret the friendships I dismissed, the foolish lies I believed, and the time I wasted.

On the other side of that season, I remember one Sunday at Watermark Community Church in Dallas when Pastor Todd Wagner brought onstage a tiger cub from a tiger refuge park. Since I was leading worship that day, I had a chance to interact with the cub off-stage. It was cute and cuddly, but months later, when Todd went to visit his friend at the park, that same white Siberian tiger was already hundreds of pounds; it was soon shipped off to a zoo because even those who raised it and fed it every day were unable to control it.

In his sermon, Todd likened the baby tiger to sin. They both start out small—cute and cuddly, if you will. There is an appeal in petting them. But eventually the tiger and the sin will grow up to eat you alive. The literal scratches I carried on my arms for the next couple of weeks reminded me of that truth.

Alienation: Sin Makes Us Strangers

One of the ways we can recognize that sin is growing in our lives is that it alienates us from our rhythms of responsibility, from those we love, and most of all from God. In 2 Samuel 11, we find David lazing in his palace bed until late into the evening and then strolling around on his roof (vv. 1–2). After years of being responsible, David had apparently decided to take a long king's vacation.

Time off is often much needed, but as we read on, we see clearly that this was more than time off—it was shirking. David should have been tending to his kingly duties, overseeing his military as they defended Israel. Instead, during his leisurely jaunt on the roof, he spotted Bathsheba bathing, and he immediately had her brought to him. He slept with her and sent her home.

This was all out of character for David. Bathsheba and the servant who accompanied her to the palace and home again must have wondered at their king's behavior.

When Bathsheba ended up pregnant, David called Uriah, her husband, home from war so it would look like Bathsheba's baby was her husband's. Uriah shows us how David should have acted. Uriah wouldn't go home for leisure, not when the nation was at war. Loyal to his army and his country, he slept outside the palace. The next day, David got him drunk in the hope that he would go home to his wife.

Upstanding Uriah still refused to go home. So on the third day, David sent him back to war carrying a note to the captain, commanding that Uriah be left vulnerable on the front line of the battle.

Who is this David? Joab, the army captain, must have wondered what had gotten into him. Uriah, the innocent one, was soon killed, and David quickly went through with a wedding to his widow.

Lives were destroyed, other people were forced to do David's dastardly deeds, and most of all, the Lord's justice was violated. In his song of repentance, David sang woefully, "Against you—you alone—I have sinned" (Ps. 51:4).

David knew he had failed God's call to love Him with heart, soul, mind, and strength and to love and honor humanity. In his state of slothfulness, he had turned his heart to his own interests and onto the path of sin, which led him further from God's voice. The shepherd-king, who had once allowed himself to be led by his Shepherd-God and who had protected and guided his people, had become a dangerous wolf—a stranger to all that was good.

Though King David's life and his place in history are quite different from ours, the story of how sin crouched at his door and broke in resonates with most of us. It sure does with me.

My most memorable season of sin began during the time when I was on the road nonstop. I left little space for worship, for true community, or for authentic, vulnerable connection with close friends. Sure, I had friends who shared my Christian perspective whom I kept in touch with, but I was careful not to tell them what I didn't want them to know.

I listened to sermons often, and I read lots of Christian books. Our crew prayed together before shows and sometimes at other times too. But when it came to intentionality with God, I was a sloth. My primary focus was work, not my friendship with Him. As a result, my priorities and perspective began to change. Soon the people most frequently speaking into my life were completely work-focused and not focusing on God at all, just like I was. Nesting comfortably in the armpit of cultural Christianity, I thought I was doing just fine.

I began to drift away from my most solid friends. I ate, slept, and breathed my career. My aim was not to be the most successful in the world—just to do my job well. So I didn't see my work ethic as out of bounds. I was missing the truth that my ultimate purpose had become work instead of honoring the One who gave me that work. Though my mind believed the words I sang every night, my heart was quickly forgetting how to trust their power. I was not excited about truth. I had become a stranger to God. My prayers were no longer personal but merely polite.

Polite Prayers

One of the things I love about the Psalms, especially those of David, is how vulnerable and brutally honest they teach us to be before

God. David never held anything back, which I take as a call for us to follow suit.

In the earliest days of my career, I had taken every decision to God. But as life grew more hectic and as things went well, I consulted Him less and less. I was drinking from a fire hose of activity. I didn't have time to discern my path forward by sitting and talking to Him through reading and prayer.

Of course, I did have time. What I did not have was the patience or desire.

I remember telling my mom several times that God had given me this career opportunity and He had also given me the mental tools to make it work. Of course, there was an ounce of truth in that. I was responsible to work hard and be wise. But had I made space for friendship with God, He would have guided me through the details.

With this attitude, my prayers morphed over time from *impassioned* to *civil*. When I prayed, it was half-hearted and without expectation that God would answer. This take on things influenced every prayer. I asked for wisdom in making business decisions and navigating difficult situations but never took time to be still and seek it out. When nothing changed, I took it as the Lord not caring about the details, and I gave up asking for wisdom. I longed to get married, but the Lord didn't seem to be answering that prayer either. So I stopped asking.

When my prayers became superficial and I no longer trusted God enough to lay before Him all my longings, I naturally began entrusting my heart to other loves.

Needless to say, this had catastrophic consequences. A couple of dating relationships I had no business being in led to breakups that reverberated through years of heartache. Work stress mounted too as I completed my record deal and tried to plan my next steps. It was all up to me, after all.

I was not who I had been before. I became a stranger to my rhythms of responsibility, my closest friends, and my most faithful Lord.

As David said, this is what we are prone to. He sang to God, "Indeed, I was guilty when I was born; I was sinful when my mother conceived me" (Ps. 51:5). In other words, our natural bent is to turn from what is good, from what God wants, to what we want. And being human and finite, we can't see the far-reaching consequences that will come as a result.

But God in His mercy never wants us to remain in that darkened state. He will wake us up any way He can. And usually He does it by sending someone to sound the alarm.

The Wake-Up Call

In 2 Samuel 12, we hear what happened after David married Bathsheba. God sent the prophet Nathan to the palace. He called David out with a heart-wrenching story of a poor man who bought a little lamb, which became his beloved family pet. Then a rich man came along and stole it and ate it for dinner instead of taking one from his numerous flocks.

David was infuriated, his passion for justice instantly ignited. Then Nathan delivered the kicker: *David* was that heartless rich man. God had given David everything, and He demanded to know why David had despised Him by believing the lie that something was missing.

Does this sound familiar? In the garden of Eden, the serpent told Eve that God was lying and that eating fruit from the beautiful, forbidden tree would merely make her as smart as God. He told her that God had forbidden it because He didn't want the competition (Gen. 3:1–5). Sin is believing the lie that God has not actually been good and has not given us what we really need. As He did with Adam and Eve in the garden, God in His justice insisted on intense consequences for David's sin. But just as He did in the garden, God showed mercy, sparing David's life.

God often communicates His love and friendship to us through care and concern from others. After Nathan delivered his word from the Lord, everything changed. The session of honest communication moved David from a mental space of lying, hiding, and sneaking around to open confession. David confessed to Nathan and then to the Lord, falling on His mercy. Often it is this sort of confrontation that helps us see that the baby tiger we should have run from in the beginning is now eating us alive.

One of my best friends, Charlynn, did this for me. We had met on day one of college, and I quickly learned that Charlynn was not only the life of the party but also a most dedicated and honest friend.

As I told her the joys and woes of the relationship I was in at the time, she boldly called me out. "What are you doing, Ginny? This is not where you should be, and you know it." Even in my post-relationship misery, she lovingly reminded me that I had brought this on myself, that I could not blame anyone else, and that it would take time to heal. She and my other closest friends rose to the task of loving me and speaking truth I needed to hear about my personal life and career.

It took a good bit of time to come out of the haze, but one of the things that helped was being accountable to these friends and people in pastoral roles. And confession brought me to see the many ways I had been wrong and helped me turn the corner toward truth. Over time, having honest people around me cleared the fog and allowed me to regain my vision.

The Transformation: Falling on Mercy

The beautiful thing we see in David's psalm is that he knew that in order to be forgiven and changed, to be released from the weight of guilt and shame, and to be able to praise again, he had to first fall on God's mercy. He cried out for the Lord to take action because he knew this was his only hope: "Be gracious to me, God, according to your faithful love; according to your abundant compassion, blot out my rebellion. Completely wash away my guilt and cleanse me from my sin" (Ps. 51:1–2).

David now knew how horrific his sin was. He knew that he deserved judgment, but he also knew that the Lord had made a covenant promise to love His people and forgive them when they turned to Him (Ex. 34:7). He knew that his sins would define him unless the Lord's love redefined him. He would never be able to do enough to cleanse himself—only the God of justice and mercy could wash him clean.

We often think we can rid our lives of sin and guilt by striving to be good. We think that somehow our good deeds can overpower our failures.

I remember a strange response I had during my dark season: I heard the noise of guilt in absolutely everything. I would pay for dinners I didn't need to pay for or go to great lengths to please people who weren't even asking. I was trying to earn my way back to feeling good about myself. And back into God's favor. As David said, my sin was ever before me (Ps. 51:3).

When I finally got the memo that my task was impossible, that only God Himself was powerful enough to wash away the dirt of sin and to silence the voices of guilt and shame, I was deeply relieved. Falling on His mercy, realizing He was my only hope, was the first step to becoming free again.

And it is the first step to staying free every day. As human beings, we prefer to try to earn freedom on our own merit. But remembering that we cannot make ourselves whole—and returning to the One who can—brings great depth to our songs.

The Transformation: Bold Prayers

David's prayer of repentance could have led to utter despair, but instead, it led to greater hope.[2] David asked God to recreate his heart and to "renew a right spirit" in him (v. 10 ESV). He begged the Lord to remain close to him, to not dismiss him. He boldly asked God to help him be willing to always do what He asked (vv. 11–12).

In other words, David knew that just as his cleansing must happen supernaturally, so must his change of heart. For David to want to honor God in the midst of prosperity—or when a beautiful woman was in front of him or when he simply would prefer to lie around in bed—would require God's Spirit to be breathing into his heart and mind.

A certain spiritual blindness comes over us when we sin. We do not think or see clearly. David wanted no more of that. Rather than simply saying to his God, "I'll do better next time," he said, "I know I won't do any better next time unless You first do a miracle in me."

Next David said something quite interesting: "Then I will teach the rebellious your ways, and sinners will return to you" (v. 13).

One of the best parts of being set free spiritually is that you can honestly share where you've been and how you've failed. Why? Because the story has (and keeps having) a miraculous ending. You have been changed. And God keeps changing you.

David had discovered how powerful the pull of sin is. He knew that pull would not completely go away, but he now knew the greater power with which he could fight his way through. He wanted others to know that power as well so sin would not darken their minds and weigh them down. The Lord answered David's prayer to teach, as generations of people for thousands of years have learned the ways of repentance from him.

I too am now eager to talk about breaking free from a misoriented life and the powerful hold of sin, guilt, and shame. Though I know my new life in Christ is not dependent on what I do, I need a constant gospel refresher. My southern "everything's okay" approach simply will not do. Instead, it's Pastor Jack Miller's words I need: "Cheer up: You're a worse sinner than you ever dared imagine, and you're more loved than you ever dared hope."[3]

I return to the truth of the cross again and again because it gives me the power to admit I'm not okay on my own. And it reminds me that, in Christ, I am being made perfect and am perfectly loved. This truth helps me turn from my self-made darkness more willingly and more quickly. And it makes me want to tell everyone so they can also be set free from what binds them up inside.

Celebration: The Practice of Praise

David asked God to restore the joy of his salvation (Ps. 51:12). One thing that gets us in big trouble is when the beauty and power of who God is and what He has done for us fade in our minds.

When we don't talk to or listen to the Lord, the idea of salvation becomes theoretical. We forget how the song goes. And this forgetting leads us to singing songs of hopelessness. But when we talk to God, reminding ourselves of His faithfulness and thanking Him for both the significant and the subtle blessings, He will restore our joy—our inner smile that remains through trials.

Our walks as believers will not be exceedingly exciting every day. Nor will we have constant courage to withstand temptation as we roam this planet. But when we are tuned to His heart, when we practice praise and thanksgiving, the thought of our salvation will bring joy as in the hour we first believed. And when we are contemplating that joy, it is much harder to believe a lesser joy might be more satisfying.

David said that when the Lord delivered him from his sin, He would also give him the power and the joy to sing again (vv. 14–15). But not only would David's *mouth* praise Him, his heart would also.

The Lord saw David's broken spirit and contrite heart as evidence of his true worship (v. 17). This is more than just a call to "stay humble"—this is a promise. God fills the humble heart with hope. He makes the broken spirit whole. Strength comes to the one who says, "My joy is found only in knowing You."

As a result, the chorus of joy that comes with repentance would continue on for David in future songs: "As far as the east is from the west, so far does he remove our transgressions from us" (Ps. 103:12 ESV).

The Bigger Story

David's lesson reverberates through history, long after his death. His people continued to sing his song of confession and repentance, though we can infer they spent many years singing it without letting its words move them to change.

After they turned away from God, He let their sins find them out, and their land was taken from them. But upon returning from exile, the Jews followed David's lead in earnestly praying Psalm 51, "Do good to Zion in your good pleasure; build up the walls of Jerusalem" (v. 18 ESV). They likely sang this psalm as they rebuilt Jerusalem and resettled in Judah, knowing they could not do this work alone. Later still, those who did not forget God or His promises continued to sing this song of lament and praise through four hundred years of darkness.

Then a greater king than David emerged to do what David could not. He Himself was tempted by Satan. But with the words written on His heart, the words of Scripture, Jesus resisted: "It is written, 'You shall worship the Lord your God and him only shall you serve'" (Matt. 4:10 ESV). Jesus had come to walk among us, not only to live a perfect life, facing down every temptation, but also to pay for our wrongs by dying on a cross. And as He did, He begged God to forgive the sin of His oppressors (Luke 23:34).

We have a greater peace than David did. We know how our sins were paid for. We walk with the One who paid for them. We are made alive, free from the darkness and heaviness of sin. Jesus has erased our certificate of debt and nailed it to the cross (Col. 2:14)!

So we live, responding in love to Christ's gift, not in order to be free but because if we belong to Him, we are already free. As the cross drives us to our knees, the truth of freedom takes root in our hearts, and we can't help but sing our freedom song, loving and forgiving as we are loved and forgiven.

Your Freedom Song

Today we know that everything is not okay in us. Every day, we do wrong. We are tempted to live under the weight of our sin, guilt, and shame. But the Lord says we can have hope and joy if we only turn and ask. Write a song of turning and running to the Lord and of His faithfulness to forgive.

Or write a song of praise for the freedom and wholeness you have found in Him. Here is a bit of inspiration for you:

> *My sin—oh the bliss of this glorious thought—*
> *My sin, not in part but the whole,*
> *Is nailed to the Cross and I bear it no more.*
> *Praise the Lord, praise the Lord, oh my soul!*[4]

God's Song of Wholeness

Let's memorize David's prayer so we too can sing it to the Lord: *"Create in me a clean heart, O God, and renew a right spirit within me" (Ps. 51:10 ESV).*

Let's also memorize Christ's words to His followers and to us about how to live in light of forgiveness: *"Whenever you stand praying, forgive, if you have anything against anyone, so that your Father also who is in heaven may forgive you your trespasses" (Mark 11:25 ESV).*

"Cry out loudly, don't hold back! Raise your voice like a trumpet. Tell My people their transgression and the house of Jacob their sins.

"They seek Me day after day and delight to know My ways, like a nation that does what is right and does not abandon the justice of their God. They ask Me for righteous judgments; they delight in the nearness of God."

"Why have we fasted, but You have not seen? We have denied ourselves, but You haven't noticed!"

"Look, you do as you please on the day of your fast, and oppress all your workers....

"Isn't this the fast I choose: To break the chains of wickedness, to untie the ropes of the yoke, to set the oppressed free, and to tear off every yoke?

"Is it not to share your bread with the hungry, to bring the poor and homeless into your house, to clothe the naked when you see him, and not to ignore your own flesh and blood?

"Then your light will appear like the dawn, and your recovery will come quickly. Your righteousness will go before you, and the LORD's glory will be your rear guard.

"At that time, when you call, the LORD will answer; when you cry out, He will say, 'Here I am.' If you get rid of the yoke among you, the finger-pointing and malicious speaking,

and if you offer yourself to the hungry, and satisfy the afflicted one, then your light will shine in the darkness, and your night will be like noonday.

"The LORD will always lead you, satisfy you in a parched land, and strengthen your bones. You will be like a watered garden and like a spring whose waters never run dry."

Isaiah 58:1–3, 6–11 HCSB

Chapter 7

God's Song of Justice and Mercy

Learning to Stand Together

All of us can point to experiences that have greatly influenced the way we see the world. Growing up in a predominantly African American school, I learned early on to value the beauty of diversity and to seek to understand our differences. I experienced firsthand the profound power of standing together—and the jarring notes of discord that reverberate when we don't.

I've known Octavia almost since I can remember. Our parents joined forces to start a support group for parents of visually impaired children, and Octavia and I were always the oldest two kids at the meetings. So we joined forces too.

A year older than me and with three younger brothers, Octavia is a force of nature, always ready with great ideas and the perfect comeback. I was glad she was usually on my side. When we were young, she had enough vision to report details I couldn't see—who was wearing the cutest dress, whose hair looked a hot mess, and who snuck the most cookies during the parent meetings.

In addition to public school, Octavia and I attended a school for blind and visually impaired students for at least part of each day. We both lived locally, but our classes were filled with kids from all over the state and from all walks of life. Those early exposures to peers with different cultures, skin colors, and life experiences shaped the way I look at the world—and the people in it.

Regardless of our differences, we all wake up every day with the same basic needs and desires: to be seen, known, and loved and to survive and thrive in the world. Knowing that God sees not only our basic needs but also our desperate need for Him, I want to see each person this way too. Because if I do, I am much quicker to move toward others and meet whatever needs of theirs I can—and far less apt to misunderstand or dismiss them.

Learning to meet others' needs—to do social justice—is at the forefront of our thinking these days. Whether we're asking how to better embrace and care for those of different races, the homeless, victims of domestic abuse, those with disabilities, or at-risk children, we are deeply passionate about these issues, defending our various positions religiously.

It's important to remember that God invented justice. His concern for the weak and unprotected puts all our petitions and protests, as well as our inaction, to shame. I confess that, in the past, I have taken His call to do justice and mercy as more of a recommendation than a command. But a command it is. One that, if ignored, should cause me to question whether I have faith at all.

Facing Adversity

During elementary school, Octavia and I discovered our mutual love of music and organized our homeroom class into a singing group.

We coerced our peers into joining, though we voted them out or suspended their memberships when we didn't like their attitudes or their singing. Sometimes we got ourselves out of classwork by entertaining our teachers with the extensive music library we could perform on the spot.

In sixth grade, when Octavia and I realized we were the only unfireable members of our group, we officially became best friends. But sometime during our middle school years, one of our teachers predicted the demise of our friendship with words that still ring in our ears.

"Y'all are close now, but when you get older, you won't be. You don't think skin color matters, but trust me, it does. Colors don't mix. Never have, never will. You'll find out the hard way sooner or later."

We promised each other she was absolutely wrong, and over our remaining school years, we learned together what friendship really meant. We saw each other through typical teen drama and more nay-saying about our friendship. I am certain all the opposition ultimately strengthened our resolve to stay close.

But it got me thinking. I literally could not see color, but I was constantly aware of the fact that other people could. I could not understand why skin color need be someone's defining characteristic. Sure, we were raised with different cultural experiences, but I thought that made friendship more colorful.

Octavia and I—and so many of our other friends—experienced growing up together, not as Black, White, or Hispanic kids but as kids. We got nervous together before varsity cheerleading competitions. We cried our eyes out together as we sang for our high school principal's funeral. We were camp counselors together and painted each other's nails when the younger kids went to bed. I learned to love and value Octavia because of who she was—my best friend. And I learned to respect her because of all the beautiful ways she was different from me.

Octavia and I eventually went our separate ways to college and beyond, but we have continued to walk with each other through the good and the dark days. Our lives look very different. She's a mom managing three, and I'm doing my best to manage myself. She doesn't have much time for singing anymore, and I still can't stop. I wish I had soul, and she actually does.

She's still Black, and I'm still White. But we value our differences as much as we value the ways we're alike. In spite of what our teacher said, our friendship has stood the test of time. And because we have learned how to walk with each other in every season, we continue to stand together now.

God's Chorus of Mercy and Justice

People often think that, in the Old Testament, God is cruel, merciless, and horribly unjust. I wish I had time to unpack all the proof that this is simply untrue. But suffice it to say that, from the beginning, the Lord's heart has always been for the poor, the broken, and the vulnerable.

So that we can better understand God's desire for justice and mercy, let's get a quick big-picture glance at God's call to the Israelites on this subject:

- When the Lord delivered the law to Moses and the
  Israelites as they were wandering around on the

way to the Promised Land, He described Himself
as the God who "executes justice for the fatherless
and the widow, and loves the [immigrant], giving
him food and clothing" (Deut. 10:18).

- He called the Israelites to love the immigrant
  too; they, after all, had been sojourners in the
  land of Egypt (Deut. 10:19).
- He laid out various ways those in need should
  be served, insisting that His people lend without
  interest (Ex. 22:25) and that they never com-
  pletely harvest their crops so the poor and the
  immigrant could eat by gathering what was left
  in the fields (Lev. 19:9–10).
- He even promised that if people obeyed the wise
  laws He had laid out for them, there would be no
  poor people among them (Deut. 15:4–5).

Over time, God's people turned away from Him and His call.
And as we've already seen, turning away from the true God leads to
a turning *toward* other gods and an unraveling of all of life.

With God's guidance, King David led the people in following
the Lord. But his son Solomon, though he had pious moments, was
more in love with his wealth and his many wives and their gods than
with the Lord. His subjects followed suit.

After Solomon's reign, God's people divided into the northern
kingdom (Israel) and the southern kingdom (Judah). The books of
Kings and Chronicles and the books of the prophets detail how the
two nations became worse than the nations around them, not only

in their atrocious pagan practices of worshipping false gods but also in how they treated one another.

The prophet Amos, for instance, sang to the northern kingdom of Israel about how God's judgment would come on them unless they turned to seek Him and stopped trampling the poor. Among other things, they were overtaxing those who could barely afford food, and they were building fancy houses for themselves with the profits (5:8–12). But the kingdom of Israel ignored Amos and did not stop mistreating their poor. So as God had promised, their wealth disappeared and they were destroyed in 722 BC at the hands of Assyria.

The kingdom of Judah lasted a bit longer, with kings sprinkled in who answered the Lord's call for true worship. But by 586 BC, after giving in to infamous practices of idol worship, unrelenting cruelty to the poor, and injustice toward the righteous, they were exiled, and Jerusalem was razed to the ground.

Isaiah prophesied not only about the exile of God's people and the destruction of their beloved Jerusalem but also about their eventual return to their land and what kind of kingdom they could enjoy if they followed the Lord's ways.[1] Through Isaiah, God opened to His people not only the glories of that kingdom to come but also what would result instead if Israel continued to live as they had in the past. In Isaiah 58, the Lord, knowing that history would repeat itself, painted a clear picture for Israel of His better way forward.

God's Problem with Religion

The Lord insisted Isaiah "cry out loudly" about His people's sins (v. 1). Though they did religious things, they were merely posing as a faithful people. The fact that they didn't "do" God's justice demonstrated the true state of their hearts. They were interested in knowing God's ways, feeling Him near, and having His justice and mercy work in their favor (vv. 1–2). They felt pretty great about their superspirituality and asked the Lord why He wasn't impressed. He replied in essence, "Even on the days you fast, you are oppressing others. Your religion stinks; your hearts and your actions are truly ugly. Why would I be moved by your fasting?" (vv. 3–4).

God's problem with the people was that they were practicing the rituals of religion, not living in light of His blessing. If they were truly worshipping Him, they would have been in awe of Him and would have been pursuing the things He loves, including justice and mercy. To not pursue justice and mercy is to not pursue God.

At the end of the chapter, God challenged His people to honor the Sabbath, to keep "from doing whatever you want on my holy day … not going your own ways, seeking your own pleasure, or talking business; then you will delight in the LORD" (vv. 13–14).

Interestingly, in God's messages via the prophets, honoring the Sabbath and meeting the needs of the oppressed are often spoken of in the same passage, as they are here. The root of the people's sin was their lack of trust in God and respect for His authority. They didn't honor His Sabbath by resting. They didn't offer His care to suffering members of their community. Instead, they served themselves, continuing to turn away from God and oppress others.

Doing True Worship

We, like the children of Israel, tend to prefer religious practices to action. We want to sit with God and feel Him near. We want to know what His will is for our lives and watch Him do fabulous things with our unique gifts. But we forget that when we belong to Him, we are given not only a beautifully unique set of gifts and resources but also direct access to His will.

God said repeatedly that a most important part of doing His will is to love the poor and needy. Not only was it a message He had Moses and the prophets sing frequently, but it was also a mission Jesus carried out and passed along to His followers. They took it literally by selling some of their possessions so that every one of their church members was provided for (Acts 2:45).

Just like those who have come before, we serve, love, and care for others because we remember how we were lost and wandering and how He rescued us and now carries us in His arms of love. To find God is not to remain on our knees, indefinitely pondering Him. It is to rise to our feet and go do what He has called us to do with the love He has given us. And as we do, He will empower us and shape our abilities in the most amazing, unexpected ways.

During my last couple of years living in Nashville, my friend Kori taught me a lot about how to worship with my actions. Her full-time gig is working with local refugees from all over the world who have been resettled in the US by NGOs. I've gotten to be involved in many of her adventures with Nashville World Outreach Partnership, but the most unexpected was when she asked if I'd help lead a Bible study for middle school girls. Most of the girls were from Burma but had been raised in a refugee camp in Thailand. I loved the idea, but I was hesitant at first. I have so little time as it is. And so much to do. But in a moment of clarity, I said yes.

On the first afternoon of the Bible study, we collected the girls from their homes into a van and headed to the apartment of one of the middle schoolers, where there was enough space for all of us. Everyone sat on the floor in a circle, sharing a big bag of clementines and some milk. We talked about the good things from the day and the hard things.

School is very difficult for most of these girls since English is their second language. Life after school is also challenging, as many of their parents work multiple jobs to have enough money for food and rent. Several of these tweens were taking care of their younger siblings till their parents got home late at night—cooking for them and helping them with their homework and then doing their own.

After we talked about those things, we laid before God our requests for protection, for strength in school, and for enough money for food. Then we studied the story of how God provided for Adam and Eve in the garden of Eden.

To close out our time, we sang several worship songs together. To hear young girls who have very little, who have been to hell and back, praising at the top of their lungs—"Bless the Lord, oh my soul, and all that is within me, bless his holy name!" (Ps. 103:1)—is an experience I don't have words for. I spent most of our worship times trying not to bawl as all the words we sang took on new meaning for me.

During that first Bible study, I felt as if the Lord were saying, "What better thing could you possibly have to do than worship here?"

Loving and serving those who have needs I don't is key to doing His will. Needless to say, middle school Bible study became a favorite part of my week until I moved away from Nashville. And when I go back, we try to get the gang together to sing and hang out. God meets me through the lives of those girls in ways He couldn't if I sat holed up in prayer by myself. As I chat, sing, and pray with them, I get a sense of God's heart for them. I wouldn't be able to see it or feel it if I weren't there.

To God, it's good to fast by denying yourself bread, but it's even better to share your bread. True worship is to deny our need to be comfortable and instead to serve others with what we have. Our time with God is of utmost importance—but if it doesn't inspire change, if it doesn't lead us to go and do, we must ask whether we're actually spending time with God with open hearts or just enjoying the quiet.

I should take a moment here to consider a thought that might be running through your mind and often runs through mine: *I can't add another thing to my life.*

"Doing" can become its own ritual, its own religion. Most of us are tired; the idea of adding something more to our to-do lists is overwhelming. But what if we saw this work as a way to commune with God? A way to worship and honor Him? A way He teaches us to see the world more clearly and know His heart more deeply?

After the Lord challenged Israel on their view of worship, He gave them a practical list of things to do. He said they should break the chains of wickedness, set the oppressed free, share bread with the hungry, bring the poor and homeless into their houses, clothe the naked, stop the finger-pointing and malicious talk, and be attentive to the people and needs around them (Isa. 58:6–7, 9).

The Lord promised that if His people would do these things, He would walk with them, answering them, giving them strength, and protecting them. And He would give them the ability to rebuild the city of Jerusalem, which then lay in ruins. Not only that, but His people themselves would also be a living, breathing, radiant example of Him. Together, they as a community would radiate God's light to the world (vv. 8–12).

Doing justice and mercy, then, is not only a way we please God; it is also how we reflect God and how we bring His hope to the world in tangible form. When we are connected to His heart for people, we are able to be His hands and feet. And for us, He brings not only clear vision but also deep satisfaction in Him as we pursue what He loves.

A couple of years ago, I visited Thailand to lead worship at a conference for Rescue:Freedom International, an organization fighting human trafficking and sexual exploitation. The attendees were partners working all over the world to free children, women, and men from slavery. I've always been a supporter of antitrafficking work in theory, but as the rescue workers shared stories from their day-to-day lives with me, I was profoundly moved.

Their work is hard. Endless risks are involved. It can take years to build trust with those who are being exploited. Sometimes the local and national governments offer no protection. The rescue workers risk their lives fighting for the freedom of the oppressed.

As they work relentlessly in the trenches, the Lord is often their only sustaining power and hope, giving them eyes for what needs to be done next and the strength to do it. Many of them told me that the endless fight for freedom would be too difficult to face each day if they did not believe it was God's mission—and the one He had called them to.

They keep going, trusting that, even in the hardest moments when they do not understand, God is in the midst of their work and will continue to sustain them every time they come to the end of their strength. I heard their faith each night as we sang of our hope together.

Jesus' Song of Justice

After Isaiah served as God's mouthpiece for justice, he told of someone who had been commissioned by God to come and free the oppressed (Isa. 61:1–2).

Hundreds of years later, Jesus stood in the synagogue in His hometown, reading to the people from that very scroll: "The Spirit of the Lord is on me, because he has anointed me to preach good news to the poor. He has sent me to proclaim release to the captives and recovery of sight to the blind, to set free the oppressed" (Luke 4:18).

He then told His captivated audience that these words of Isaiah had been fulfilled in their hearing (v. 21). God's Son came not only to deliver us from our captivity to fear, guilt, and shame but also to demonstrate how to live the heart of God by doing all those things literally.

Jesus took this Old Testament message a step further. He said that when we serve others—first and foremost, fellow believers—we are serving Him personally. Anticipating what He will say on the last day to those who followed Him, Jesus gave this list:

> I was hungry and you gave me food, I was thirsty
> and you gave me drink, I was a stranger and you
> welcomed me, I was naked and you clothed me,
> I was sick and you visited me, I was in prison and
> you came to me…. As you did it to one of the
> least of these my brothers, you did it to me. (Matt.
> 25:35–36, 40 ESV)

In other words, those receiving the gift of the kingdom of God were those whose love for God motivated them to care for their brothers and sisters in Christ who were in need. Each time they had done so, they had metaphorically cared for Jesus' physical needs. They were not doing this to *earn* favor, but their acts of mercy showed that they belonged to Him.[2]

We hear Jesus continue the Lord's call for justice and mercy, and we see in the Gospels how He lived it out each day of His life. But where and how do *we* answer this call? Where do we begin?

The Bigger Story

In Galatians 6:10, Paul exhorted the church to "do good to all people, especially to those who belong to the family of believers" (NIV).

In the early centuries of Christianity, the Roman world could not make sense of this odd religion and its practices. Women, especially widows—who had no clout in society—not only made up the majority of the church population but also played important roles in its care ministries.[3] Perhaps most perplexing to outsiders was Christians' robust love and care for one another and for the general public.

The fourth-century emperor Julian said in a letter, "It is disgraceful that, when no Jew ever has to beg, and the impious Galilaeans [Christians] support not only their own poor but ours as well, all men see that our people lack aid from us."[4] Those who didn't have God had no reason to be generous. But both God and His Son insist that we radiate love through our actions.

Before we think about serving the wide world, let's consider serving those right under our noses. Serving Jesus means serving members of His local body first and foremost. Quite frankly, the idea of contributing money to organizations working on the other side of the world or getting a group together to serve at a soup kitchen across town is a much sexier proposition than serving the poor, needy, and often annoying right here among us. There's nothing wrong (and everything right) with serving those who are far away, for sure. But let's address our immediate, body-of-Christ neighbors first.

Who is your neighbor? I am, for one.

If you didn't know me and you met me trying to find my way into your church building or walking down your street with my white cane, how would you treat me? To avoid the awkwardness, would you turn tail and run when I came your direction? Or would you say hi and ask if I needed help?

Would you be interested in being my friend?

If you tend to avoid awkward, unknown, or difficult people, you are not alone. I often have the same reaction until I check myself. I don't want to care for those whose challenges might take my precious time either.

But there is a key message in God's song through Isaiah and also in Jesus' songs: take care of your own—those who are in need in your local body of believers. Jesus' brother James said to the church, "Listen, my dear brothers and sisters: Didn't God choose the poor in this world to be rich in faith and heirs of the kingdom that he has promised to those who love him?" (James 2:5).

Jesus sang this same beautiful news: the poor and the meek are the ones who are given the keys to the kingdom (Matt. 5:3, 5). When we are "rich," we perceive that we have control over our lives and we sense our need for God less. But those who have little have less trouble seeing their need and their inability to make it on their own.

Trusting God is easier when we know we can't trust ourselves. Those who have less often have a wiser perspective on the world and their need for God. That's why we should not only serve them but also learn from them. And those receiving service can accept help with grace and love.

But don't miss the other key truth here: Christianity ignores class distinctions. It doesn't matter who you are, where you've come from, or what your financial status is—everyone is equal in the body of Christ. That includes both the giver and the receiver of aid.

I have been exceedingly blessed to live a very full life. But I know many folks with physical, emotional, or financial challenges who live unbelievably isolated lives. And I have certainly tasted this pain in many seasons. Many of those who, because of ongoing needs, live in isolation don't always respond well to love. They haven't had the opportunity to learn how.

So if you meet someone at church who could use help finding a seat or paying for food, do not have pity on her. Instead, invite her into your circle. It will make all the difference in her life and yours. Why? Here's a singing analogy that might help.

During high school choral competitions, our one-hundred-voice concert choir would often link arms or pinkie fingers as we performed. The physical connection helped us breathe together, stop together, and match pitch. It was unifying, and it usually made us successful in competitions.

Serving is not merely doing *for* others, though that is part of it. It is singing the good news of Jesus to them until they are able to sing along with you. In other words, serving in Jesus' way means pouring life and power into each other so that we are able to pour into the world.

Some Christians are seen and known only by their service—it defines them. Others are defined by their need to be served. But each of us needs to serve and be served in different ways, and standing together, being united in Christ's love, is the only way to create a beautiful chorus. Then we, by God's grace, can effectively serve the world in His name.

During my time as a worship leader at a church in Nashville, I got involved in several small groups. Many folks had never met a blind person before, but bonds formed as we embarked on the adventure of becoming friends. One wonderful retired couple, who are busier than most working people I know, regularly offered me rides to church events. During our conversations, I learned about the Next Door, a treatment program for women recovering from addictions. Soon enough, I was joining them frequently for trips to spend time with the ladies, singing, bringing morning devotions, and hearing their stories.

This couple's service to me within the church led me to serve others outside our church. It was incredibly meaningful work to be doing with friends. We got to see Jesus at work in each other's lives as well as in the lives of others.

Church is also where I met my good friend Kori, who invited me into all kinds of wonderful adventures with refugees. I continue to be amazed by how building relationships with my neighbors not only helps me love and serve them but also helps me catch a vision of how to serve the world beyond our immediate circle.

Serving others is a one-step-at-a-time process. The best place to start is to ask God to open your eyes to whom and how you might serve. You could ask your pastors or other church members about needs they know of among your members. Or you could go over to the person across the room who looks as if he needs a friend and simply be that friend.

Whatever our starting point or our next step may be, loving and serving—and singing through the process—works only when we reflect on how *we* have been deeply loved and cared for. Because Jesus loved us enough to live a perfect, humble life and die in our place, we are free to love others through our actions, first within our church community, and then beyond.

Paul insisted that, instead of living to please ourselves, we live to build up our neighbors. Not out of religious duty. Not even to try to please God. But with a song of remembrance and reflection in our souls: Christ, the king of all, lived not to please Himself but to carry our pain (see Rom. 15:1–3). In light of the cross, we can eagerly carry the cares of others. What could possibly reflect the gospel more?

Your Song of Justice and Mercy

Today, as we reflect on God's heart for those in need and Jesus' physical demonstration of God's heart, I can think of several songs we could write. One would be a prayer for eyes to see the needs around us and for hearts that are so moved by Jesus' love for us that we become eager and empowered to meet those needs. Or maybe you're already passionate about a cause or a need and you want to lament and plead with God for a solution. Whatever the case, here are some lyrics to get you started:

> *Take my life and let it be*
> *Consecrated, Lord, to Thee.*
> *Take my moments and my days;*
> *Let them flow in endless praise.*

> *Take my voice and let me sing*
> *Always, only for my King.*
> *Take my lips and let them be*
> *Filled with messages from Thee.*[5]

Singing God's Song

To remember how God has rescued us, let's memorize His words to Israel: *"If you offer yourself to the hungry, and satisfy the afflicted one, then your light will shine in the darkness, and your night will be like noonday. The LORD will always lead you, satisfy you in a parched land, and strengthen [you]* (Is. 58:10–11).

And let's memorize Jesus' words to us, His followers: *"The King will say to those on his right, 'Come, you who are blessed by my Father, inherit the kingdom prepared for you from the foundation of the world. For I was hungry and you gave me food, I was thirsty and you gave me drink, I was a stranger and you welcomed me, I was naked and you clothed me, I was sick and you visited me, I was in prison and you came to me'" (Matt. 25:34–36 ESV).*

My God, my God, why have you forsaken me? Why are you so far from saving me, from the words of my groaning?

O my God, I cry by day, but you do not answer, and by night, but I find no rest.

Yet you are holy, enthroned on the praises of Israel.

In you our fathers trusted; they trusted, and you delivered them....

But I am a worm and not a man, scorned by mankind and despised by the people....

Be not far from me, for trouble is near, and there is none to help....

I am poured out like water, and all my bones are out of joint; my heart is like wax; it is melted within my breast....

For dogs encompass me; a company of evildoers encircles me; they have pierced my hands and feet....

They divide my garments among them, and for my clothing they cast lots.

But you, O LORD, do not be far off! O you my help, come quickly to my aid!

Deliver my soul from the sword....

I will tell of your name to my brothers; in the midst of the congregation I will praise you....

From you comes my praise.

Psalm 22:1–4, 6, 11, 14, 16, 18–20, 22, 25 ESV

Chapter 8

A Lament for the Broken World

Can We Sing in Sorrow?

We live in a broken world. The evidence of it is all around us, not least in how it leaves us brokenhearted. Sometimes the sadness is crushing, leading us to question why terrible things happen and where God is when they do. We think either He is not there or He has turned His back on us, or maybe we aren't clever enough or good enough to find Him in our darkest moments.

But what if He *is* there? What if hope can grow even in the deepest darkness? I want to explore Psalm 22 with you. It's a lament spoken by David and then by Christ—a cry for God in the most desperate hour. We will discover how this cry led David to praise and what it meant for him and us when the same cry came from Christ's lips.

But first, so you can hear such a lament in today's terms, I want to share with you a deep sadness from my own life, knowing you likely have a similar story in yours.

Gone Too Soon

I still can't believe it's true, but the page before me says so:

> On April 27, 2014, Heaven gained another angel,
> Christi Griggs Dippel, 41, of Sherwood, Arkansas
> went to be with her Savior after a courageous battle
> with brain cancer....
>
> Christi spent most of her adult life caring for
> other people's children as if they were her own. She
> was a devoted wife, mother, daughter, sister and
> friend.
>
> Christi loved music, scrapbooking, camping
> and observing nature. She was a lifelong follower
> of Christ.... Christi lived her life by the greatest
> commandments: "Love the Lord your God with
> all your heart, all your soul and all your mind and
> love your neighbor as yourself." She always put the
> needs of others ahead of her own. We look forward
> to the day when we will see her again in Heaven.[1]

As I write this, it's been six years since we lost Christi, and the
wave of sadness that rises in me is as piercing as if it had happened
yesterday. Death is a part of life.

But it was never supposed to be.

Everyone has a hero. Mine was Christi. My only girl cousin on
my dad's side, Christi was not just three years older but infinitely
wiser and kinder than I. She was all the things I am not but aspire to
be. She possessed a nature so easy and engaging, so true and gentle,

that everyone easily called her "friend." I knew even as a young girl that Christi was a different sort. Most people who are utterly good are boring and inaccessible, but she was not. Her goodness brought light to everything. Her subtlety and gentleness drew the world in with a magnetism usually reserved for charismatic leaders.

My earliest memories with Christi are of singing together around our nana's piano or with the radio in the guest bedroom of our grandparents' cozy little house. She was a songbird with a voice so hauntingly pure, every melody lingered in the mind long after the notes had faded from the air. We usually kept a cassette recorder nearby to capture the magic.

Even though we lived hours apart—she in Little Rock and I in Jackson—we loved the same things, especially music. Our voices harmonized perfectly, and during each visit, we would simply pick up where we had left off, harmonizing our way through pop hits and worship songs. Though our meetups at Nana's were far less frequent than I would have liked, the fun we had filled me with enough courage to last until the next visit. No matter what nonsense was going on at school, time with Christi made it all seem fleeting and foolish. Her positive presence always pointed me toward the better days to come.

Christi and I sent tapes (yes, cassettes) to each other via mail (yes, snail mail). Each held ramblings about our lives and some karaoke singing of our favorite songs by REO Speedwagon, Amy Grant, or the Jets. From Christi, I learned about great bands, the mysteries of boys, and cool lipstick colors. And also what it meant to become a beautiful and kind teenager.

In the moment, I forgot most of those lessons, but I clearly remember them now. The true friendship and encouragement of my older cousin gave me a certain confidence to face the big, scary world with humility and love. A confidence I sense as deeply now as I did when I was ten.

We grew older, and our visits became less frequent. By the time I went off to college, Christi was getting married. I started going on the road, and she started having kids. But any time we talked, we picked up right where we had left off. And boy, do I wish it had been more often.

To celebrate her fortieth birthday, Christi and her friend Mandy came to Nashville to CMA Fest, a popular summer country-music fair. It was our first quality time together in ages. As always, our last meeting might as well have been the day before. We talked music, solved the world's problems, and giggled hysterically about I don't even know what. Being together took me back to those childhood music marathons, and I missed them so much.

As the girls took their leave, Christi and I promised to stay in touch more. And so we did. Our texts and phone chats were the deepest conversations we would have as adults. I wondered why we hadn't been doing it all along, and I knew it was entirely my fault.

Summer quickly faded to fall, and our time together faded into the background. In October I got the call: Christi had been diagnosed with brain cancer. They would operate first on the tumors and then do several rounds of chemo and radiation. I was in complete shock. What was happening? What was God thinking?

During that season, Christi wrote beautifully in blog posts about all that was going on. Even her texts and our phone chats were full of hope. Doctors soon removed several of her tumors and started her treatments. With every step, Christi remained positive.

The outcome was uncertain, but she was willing to be thankful for every piece of good news along the way. She didn't take any moment for granted.

She and Mandy came to Nashville again. This time, among our adventures was a trip to the studio to record a song for my upcoming album—an old hymn with an exquisite, hopeful lyric and a dark, minor melody.

> *O the deep, deep love of Jesus,*
> *Vast, unmeasured, boundless, free!*
> *Rolling as a mighty ocean*
> *In its fullness over me!*[2]

Chemotherapy had brought a slight hoarseness to Christi's angelic voice, which only made it more hauntingly beautiful. She sang melody, declaring the love she wholeheartedly believed was hers. I recorded my harmonies later so she wouldn't have to listen to me fight through tears as I sang.

Christi and her family made a couple of other visits to Nashville that year, which was glorious. But the last time I saw her, it was back in Jackson for our nana's funeral.

My time with Christi ended much as it began in childhood. But instead of tapes via snail mail, there were texts and audio files. She would text what was going on with her and ask how I was doing. Her last text was asking when my next album, the one with our song, would release. After that, there was silence. Hospice. Five days after my birthday and eighteen days before hers, Christi passed away.

Weep and Ask Why

What do you do when the world crashes down, horribly and unfairly, around you?

As a culture, we have a whole host of ways we respond to suffering, but *lament* tends to not be one of them, even for the Christian. Josh Larsen helpfully wrote that "lament isn't giving up, it's giving over. When we lift up our sorrow and our pain, we turn it over to the only one who can meet it: our God."[3]

But instead of giving our pain over to God, we shut out the noise of what is wrong and broken. We turn to entertainment or busyness or substances. We do not go to God, perhaps because we do not know how. We are confused by why a good God would allow horrible atrocities, and we don't know how to talk to Him about it. Or we write off tragedies as simply another of God's great mysteries. And we dismiss our aching souls and drown out our nagging questions with the drone of daily life.

I did, for sure. Right after Christi's funeral, I went home and started to prepare for a weekend of leading worship in Florida. I remember sobbing as I rehearsed each song in the set, wondering how on earth I would lead four services. I tried coaching myself with platitudes—Christi was in a better place, after all; the Lord was in control, after all. In the end, the only way I could get through the weekend was to avoid that tender place of tears and questions.

When I returned home, I wanted to keep pushing down the pain, but I began to let the sadness be my companion. It came in waves at the most unexpected times. At first I dreaded every moment of it and tried to fight it off with distractions. But in time

I understood that the tears had to fall. The waves of sadness from missing someone I love had to crash over me.

Even now there are days when they do. I didn't know then what I know now: the song of lament is one we must sing on our way to hope. Authentic joy rarely comes until we have allowed ourselves to taste true sorrow.

King David taught us this in many of his psalms. He lived an incredibly colorful life. As a man after God's own heart, he experienced seasons of great blessing and larger-than-life victories, but he also faced deep, dark, troubling times. As a musician and poet, David eloquently expressed his heart during every season. In suffering, he did not stuff the pain away but lamented before God.

In Psalm 22, David shows us that lament is pouring out our tears and questions to the Lord in the darkness—trusting that He hears us whether we hear Him or not. "My God, my God, why have you forsaken me? Why are you so far from saving me, from the words of my groaning? O my God, I cry by day, but you do not answer, and by night, but I find no rest" (vv. 1–2 ESV).

David was in a dark place. Literal enemies were pursuing him with a vengeance, as were the agony and fears in his own mind. We don't know the details of this season, but we do know that he had been crying out continually to God and hearing no answer. In this song, David woefully told the Lord about every circumstance, thought, and feeling—perhaps for the hundredth time.

David begged to know why. Why God seemed far away. Why He had turned His back on David in his time of need and despair. David knew that God deserves praise and that his ancestors had received help when they prayed to and trusted Him. But David hadn't. God's distance left him disoriented and discouraged, feeling like a worm, despised by everyone (vv. 1–6).

David told the Lord how his enemies talked about him, making fun of him because he believed in God (vv. 7–8). He said God *made* him trust, even as a little child (v. 9). Yet trusting God had brought him to this place of physical and emotional weakness, to the point of death. "I am poured out like water, and all my bones are out of joint; my heart is like wax; it is melted within my breast" (v. 14 ESV). Exhausted and emotionally wrecked, David was broken in every way.

So he took his struggles to the Lord. Not politely, but with brutal honesty. Behind this lament is David's awareness that he wasn't telling the God of the universe anything He didn't already know. It is because he knew that God is the only One who could change his circumstances that he cried, moaned, and wailed before Him.

During the final season of Christi's life, I asked "Why?" so often. For my own heart but even more for her husband, John, and two amazing kids, Emily and Andrew. It all seemed so unfair. And God seemed to be silent.

As I read back through our text messages, I see the simple way in which Christi, like David, lamented. She was infinitely positive, but when things began to get worse, she acknowledged it.

In mid-February she said, "Oh my word, I'm ninety years old. Using Nana's cane around the house and I'm exhausted. Praying through this." Her next text was "The most exciting thing about my day besides getting to worship in my living room thanks to online church … is that I'm awaiting my MSG-free salad with Ranch from Jason's Deli. Yum!" A few days later, she said, "I'm having to go to

PT, I've lost so much muscle. Started PT today and have been using a wheelchair some. Frowny face. Love you."

She spoke of every loss and every heartache with the awareness that there was a heavenly Father listening and love to be experienced.

A year after her passing, I got to see Christi's family during a trip to Little Rock. It was so fantastic to spend time with them but so heart-wrenching too. Again I asked God why He would leave a young family without their mother and wife.

I still ask.

I lament for Emily and Andrew, whose social media posts and text messages reflect that they have grown up to be as kind and generous and wonderful as their mom. I lament that Christi is not here to see it happening. I ask God why it is this way. I know He knows why, but I do not know. So sometimes I still wrestle with all that is wrong in this story.

Jesus Wept

When I find myself facing something terribly grievous and unfair, I always come back to the story of Jesus as He grieved the loss of His friend Lazarus.

In John 11, we hear the account. Lazarus's sisters, Mary and Martha, had sent Jesus a message that their brother was ill, but Jesus waited two days to go to them. He even said that Lazarus's illness would not end in death but was for the glory of God (v. 4). When He finally set out for Judea, He told His disciples, "Our friend Lazarus has fallen asleep, but I go to awaken him" (v. 11 ESV). When they didn't get it, He clarified: "Lazarus has died, and for your sake I am glad that I was not there, so that you may believe. But let us go to him" (vv. 14–15 ESV).

Jesus reached Bethany, and Martha immediately came to Him, insisting with despair, "Lord, if you had been here, my brother wouldn't have died" (v. 21). Jesus told her, "Your brother will rise again" (v. 23).

Although He knew what He was about to do, when Mary and her friends and family came to Him weeping, Jesus "was deeply moved in his spirit and greatly troubled. And he said, 'Where have you laid him?' They said to him, 'Lord, come and see.'" After that, we're told simply that Jesus wept (vv. 33–35 ESV).

Even as Jesus prepared to raise Lazarus from the dead, He Himself lamented death. As Timothy Keller said, Jesus "is one with us. He feels the horrific power of death and the grief of love lost."[4]

This gives me hope in my lamenting. Whether in the loss of someone close, in the frustration of my disability, or in the times when God seems so far away, I know He loves me. I know He loves those whose suffering I'm weeping over. And not only that, but He Himself came to earth to experience the agony of death and to weep with us.

Call Him to Come

In his time of trouble and despair, David begged God to intervene—to save him from his enemies (vv. 19–21). There was in David a desperate longing for God to do something so that things would no longer be the way they were.

But we also hear in David's words an equally desperate cry for God to simply be near because trouble was near (v. 11). Just as a child needs a parent in the midst of a storm, King David, who loved to seek

God's face, needed to feel his Shepherd-God close. He needed the assurance of God's presence more than he needed things to be fixed.

Sometimes this is where our prayers ring false. We complain without asking the Lord to come near. We talk endlessly without inviting Him into our struggles. I have several journals of such one-sided prayers. Reading back through, I am amazed at how much I cried at God without engaging Him. The difference between lament and total despair is the invitation for God to come be with us. To intervene in our hearts even if He doesn't intervene in our circumstances.

At our church, we have a Sunday each month when we set aside time for corporate lament. We have cried out to God about injustice. About the plight of the poor, the orphan, and victims of domestic violence. And for all the families losing loved ones during the coronavirus pandemic. I once led us in a lament for those with disabilities and chronic illness. We know in theory that God sees and cares, but when we collectively groan and grieve before God because things are not as they should be, calling on Him to be with us and to bring change, we are following David's lead.

We live in a broken world. God wants our hearts to see and grieve that brokenness. To take it seriously and petition Him about it. To plead for healing, whether it seems on the horizon or not. And to seek His face … until our lament becomes praise.

End in Praise

In Psalm 22, as in so many other psalms, David moved from crying out in agony to erupting in praise. According to his song, the Lord had not hidden His face from him but had heard when he cried to Him (v. 24). God Himself had given David the strength to praise

Him before the great congregation, and David insisted that they praise along with him. He then declared that all the world would join in (vv. 22–31).

This could be one of those cases when, as David poured out his heart, the Spirit of the Lord finally whispered to him, igniting joy. Or it could be that David chose to praise before anything good happened.[5] Either way, by the end of his lament, David was exuberantly declaring, "They shall come and proclaim his righteousness to a people yet unborn, that he has done it" (v. 31 ESV). You and I must often think and pray our way to praise too.

My cousin Christi also taught me much about the practice of praise. In every part of her storm, she thanked the Lord for the small things. The time with her kids and husband. The hours of napping and streaming worship services. "Sometimes it may feel like you can't possibly find something good in a bad situation," she wrote in a blog, "but I remind myself right away that my huge loving God who created the universe and every detail of how my brain works, promises us that all things work together for the good of those who love Him, and I do love and trust Him through this situation."

Christi's praise exploded over everyone she met. She was full of praise, whether with the little old ladies receiving cancer treatment next to her or backstage at concerts where she told her story to artists whose music had inspired her. Christi shed tears and shared stories of God's goodness. Though she was fighting a fierce battle with brain cancer, she continually found new reasons to praise God.

I'm not as quick to praise as Christi was. I like to rehash my woes to God many times before celebrating His goodness. Because of my tendency toward anxiety, I've had to learn a path to praise that I can continually take. I've found much help in another lament, Psalms 42 and 43.

As the psalmist poured out his woes and longings to the Lord, he stopped three times to preach to his own soul, "Why, my soul, are you downcast? Why so disturbed within me? Put your hope in God, for I will yet praise him, my Savior and my God" (42:5, 11; 43:5 NIV). It's as if the lamenter was saying, "I don't feel this now, but I know it's true. So I will speak what my mind believes until my heart catches up and explodes in praise."

When we gathered for Christi's going-home service, the church was packed with more than a thousand of her friends. We cried as we read some of her beautiful writing. We thanked the Lord for her life, and we praised God for the hope that we would see her again.

But why? Why was Christi's writing not sappy and superficial self-comfort? Why was our praise in the midst of our tears real? How can thinking people hold the view that hope transcends the sorrow of death?

The Bigger Story

The Lord promised David that, no matter what, His steadfast love would never be taken away from him—his kingdom would last forever (2 Sam. 7:15–16). But David's descendants turned away from the Lord. God Himself lamented His people's hardened hearts. Through the prophets, He lamented their sin and even the consequences they must face because of it. He promised to send a suffering servant, a despised and rejected one, acquainted with grief. This servant would be pierced for sins, and by His wounds many would be healed (Isa. 53:3–5).

When Jesus came into the world, many people, even His disciples, expected He would be their earthly king, delivering the Jews from Roman rule. On many occasions, He expressed to His followers that this was not how it would go down. But they forgot or dismissed the suffering-servant portion of Isaiah's text.

The night before Jesus' death, the disciples had no idea what was coming. But Jesus knew. In the garden of Gethsemane, He lamented to Peter, James, and John, "My soul is very sorrowful, even to death; remain here, and watch with me" (Matt. 26:38 ESV). They slept while He cried to His Father three times for the curse of sin and death not to be His to carry. But surrendering His will, He said, "My Father, if this [cup] cannot pass unless I drink it, your will be done" (v. 42).

The curse of death was His to bear. There was no other way. David received relief from his enemies and vindication after being mocked. But Jesus, God's Son, was mocked and a crown of thorns thrown on His head (27:27–31). And God was silent.

Then Jesus was crucified, and the soldiers cast lots for His garments, just as David prophetically lamented (v. 35; Ps. 22:18).[6] The religious leaders scorned Him and said, "He trusts in God; let God deliver him now, if he desires him" (Matt. 27:43 ESV; Ps. 22:8). But unlike in David's psalm, there was no deliverance from heaven—only silence. Then, as Matthew tells us, "about the ninth hour Jesus cried out with a loud voice, saying, 'Eli, Eli, lema sabachthani?' that is, 'My God, my God, why have you forsaken me?'" (Matt. 27:46 ESV; Ps 22:1).

David began his lament with those words. Jesus stepped into death with those words. Separated from His Abba, Jesus cried out in agony. Not because of the horrific pain of crucifixion and imminent death, but because His beloved Father did not answer, allowing Jesus to "experience the full force of the meaninglessness of the fallen world."[7] *Our* lament can end in praise because Jesus' lament did not. The Lord did not come near but let Him carry our sin to His death.

David felt forsaken. Jesus, in the mystery and miracle of the cross, was forsaken. Darkness came. The temple curtain was ripped in two. The earth shook. Only broken hearts and dashed hopes remained. And God was silent. Until the third day, when light broke into darkness once and for all.

"The lament of Good Friday was answered three days later with the empty tomb. The greatest injustice in history became the greatest display of divine mercy. Tragedy became triumph. Lament was the voice in between."[8] His death led to resurrection. The darkness Jesus faced led to our eternal hope and light.

As D. A. Carson said, "Here is the undoing of death, the destruction of sin; Christ's resurrection is the firstfruits of the mighty resurrection that will mock the death of death and inaugurate a new heaven and a new earth." And the Christian gets to live his life by this resurrection power.[9] God answered David's cry and our cry by allowing His Son to be the despised and afflicted One in our place (Ps. 22:24).

But, oh, the joy when He was raised to life! David called all nations and future generations to praise; Christ delivered the nations by the power of His blood. Hebrews 2:9 expresses the glorious news: "We see him who for a little while was made lower than the angels, namely Jesus, crowned with glory and honor because of the suffering of death, so that by the grace of God he might taste death for everyone" (ESV).

Hebrews tells us that not only did Jesus taste death for us, but He now also sings to God together with us, just as David sang: "I will tell of your name to my brothers; in the midst of the congregation I will sing your praise" (Heb. 2:12 ESV; Ps. 22:22 ESV).[10]

This means we can sing even in our deepest sorrows … because death has been overcome. Even when we are hopeless, we can trust that hope is endless. The One who faced ultimate sorrow and death and conquered them sings to us and with us. Even in the darkness, our hearts can echo Christi's song: "How can I keep from singing His praise? I can't. He is such a good God and He loves us so much!"

Your Song of Lament

Take some time today to write your song of lament. What currently has your heart aching? What do you long for the Lord to make right? Write your song about it, inviting Him into the midst of your pain. It's okay to leave things this way, waiting for the answer of His comfort. But you can also practice praise, speaking what you know is true until your heart embraces it. Here is a song to inspire your creativity:

> *We will sing, we'll sing in the darkness*
> *With Your light, Your light here among us—*
> *Let our voices rise*
> *Through the trials of the night.*
> *We will sing of Your great love—*
> *Sing of Your great love.*[11]

Singing God's Song

Sometimes we don't have the words to pray—especially when things are difficult. Let's memorize these words from David so we can call on the Lord in this way: *"You, O LORD, do not be far off! O you my help, come quickly to my aid!" (Ps. 22:19 ESV).*

Let's also memorize Jesus' comforting words—words Christi texted to me during the last days of her life: *"I have told you these things, so that in me you may have peace. In this world you will have trouble. But take heart! I have overcome the world" (John 16:33 NIV).*

Rejoice in the Lord always. I will say it again: Rejoice! Let your graciousness be known to everyone. The Lord is near. Don't worry about anything, but in everything, through prayer and petition with thanksgiving, present your requests to God. And the peace of God, which surpasses all understanding, will guard your hearts and minds in Christ Jesus.

Finally brothers and sisters, whatever is true, whatever is honorable, whatever is just, whatever is pure, whatever is lovely, whatever is commendable—if there is any moral excellence and if there is anything praiseworthy—dwell on these things. Do what you have learned and received and heard from me, and seen in me, and the God of peace will be with you....

I have learned to be content in whatever circumstances I find myself. I know how to make do with little, and I know how to make do with a lot. In any and all circumstances I have learned the secret of being content—whether well fed or hungry, whether in abundance or in need. I am able to do all things through him who strengthens me.

Philippians 4:4–9, 11–13

Chapter 9

A Song of Inner Peace

Singing Contentment

As a kid, I was the ultimate worrywart. My three greatest fears were nuclear war with Russia (a side effect of being a child of the eighties), the possibility that during a storm I'd be struck by lightning in my bed (inspired by a horrific tale from my elementary school science teacher), and the possibility that my mom wouldn't return safely from wherever she'd gone and we'd be stuck with the babysitter for the rest of our natural lives.

Such enormous woes for such a small human.

Mom always encouraged me to lay my burdens down and go play outside. I did notice that my neighborhood cohort seemed to be carefree, so I strove to keep my worries to myself, playing ferociously in an attempt to drown them out. Still, they droned on.

Music helped me process the thoughts racing around in my mind. Working out songs on the piano brought peace like nothing else did, and I began composing my own lyrics and melodies to reason through my fears.

I often found myself singing that Jesus was always there, even when I was feeling anxious or alone. This truth would work its way into my soul as I wrote. I'd begin with a verse about some situation that was weighing down my young heart, and I'd instinctively move into the chorus with hope that the God who is always faithful would come to the rescue. I would come away from my writing time with a song that overpowered the noise in my mind.

How do *you* overpower the noise in your mind? What is your secret to finding inner peace and contentment? Our culture says we will find them when we look deep inside ourselves and surrender to the personal truth waiting there.

I'm not convinced. I am, at my core, a mass of inconsistencies and contradictions—a ball of joy and anger, courage and nerves, love and hate. My level of peace depends largely on how much sleep I got, what I ate for dinner, and how I feel I'm measuring up to everyone else. Though I know the value of hearing out my inner voice, I would be a fool to let it prescribe my path. How about you?

If contentment doesn't come from within, where do we find it? Those of us who have been Christians for a while will instinctively say it's supposed to come from knowing and resting in Christ. But if we're honest, we don't do this so well. Our era of high-stress "get all you can" living leaves us wanting, with little time and space for cultivating contentment.

The apostle Paul had much to say that can help.

From his prison cell, he wrote to the Philippians, insisting that peace was possible, regardless of circumstances. And he declared to them that he had learned the secret of being content in every situation (4:12). Though this portion of Scripture is not a song, per se, we know that Paul often sang, even in prison (Acts 16:25).

I imagine Paul singing about the secret to true peace and contentment from his jail cell. And if he could sing such a hopeful song from such a dark place, surely he can teach us how to do the same.

As we open Paul's meditation in Philippians 4, I will also share how this passage has taught me to find peace and contentment.

When Life's Noise Reaches a Fever Pitch

Years down the road, I began to understand how Paul's practice of singing the truth of Christ in every circumstance was the secret to peace in any place. But in the meantime, although my music helped, the noise around and inside me was always louder than my songs of hope. The peace they gave me was short-lived, soon overwhelmed by my worries.

By middle and high school, my fears had moved from nuclear war to the kids cursing at my cane and me in the school halls and my self-imposed pressure to succeed at cheerleading and track. (Yes, I ran track and was a cheerleader, often the top of the pyramid. I had a sighted running partner for most races, and I memorized specific techniques for doing jumps as well as the steps of the cheer routines.) I ran varsity track for five years, but I had an overpowering sense of dread before every starting gun went off, and I finally gave it up.

I began to stress over schoolwork after a teacher told my mom that though I wasn't the smartest kid in class, my work ethic made up for my lesser intelligence.

And though I loved music most of all, whenever I performed in front of an audience, I felt like I might throw up. Every time, I'd promise never to put myself through such agony again.

When I signed a record deal and began a new life of full-time travel, my anxiety came along for the ride. A couple of turbulent flights early on resulted in years of pre-trip sleepless nights. And during the early seasons of road life, singing in front of strangers was always accompanied by an extreme case of nerves. As a homebody and an introvert, new venues and new people every day exhausted me. After a few shows in a row, I'd find myself running out of words during conversations with kind fans or the friendly concert promoters hosting me, which brought on yet more anxiety.

Other aspects of work caused worry too. A well-meaning member of my record label staff told me early on, "Ginny, the only time your blindness is really noticeable is when you're onstage. We have to fix that." The words reverberated in my mind as I worked with performance coaches to figure out a way to not appear blind.

Also simmering in my mind was the understanding that, in order to remain successful, I'd have to keep releasing hit radio singles. I knew these realities were part of the life I had signed up for, but that didn't make them any easier to swallow. Somehow, I continued forward, singing about the hope, freedom, and peace I had found and knew were possible for everyone. But the words I was singing were being overpowered, drowned out by the noise in my mind.

After several years of sleepless nights and relentless anxiety, I reached out for help. A counselor and good friend insisted I go see a doctor to talk about whether I needed something more than willpower and prayer. After a long chat about my years of chronic worry and my current anxiety about work, the doctor prescribed a sleep aid and antidepressants.

Being able to sleep again was glorious, and the other medication took the edge off, but the underlying unrest lingered.

Finally the noise inside me reached a fever pitch. My life sounded more like a melancholy country or emo ballad than a song of hope and peace. A relationship ended and left me reeling. And when

Rocketown Records, my label, closed its doors, I chose to venture out to find my way as an independent musician.

Most disconcerting of all was my mom's breast cancer diagnosis that I talked about in chapter 3. Since I had a job that could be done from anywhere with an airport and since my brother, JD, a Marine Corps officer, was stationed overseas, I moved home to be with Mom during her surgery and treatments.

After Mom was finally declared cancer-free, I returned to Nashville and jumped back into writing, teaching, and traveling. But I couldn't turn down the volume of anxiety's noise, no matter the dose of meds or number of prayers.

Peace in Any Place

During that time, I began to dig through the Bible with a new resolve to unearth words of hope. I discovered a call from the apostle Paul:

> Do not be anxious about anything, but in every situation, by prayer and petition, with thanksgiving, present your requests to God. And the peace of God, which transcends all understanding, will guard your hearts and your minds in Christ Jesus. (Phil. 4:6–7 NIV)

The weight of Paul's words struck me. Don't be anxious about anything? Was that even possible?

I read further and found this: "I have learned the secret of being content in any and every situation, whether well fed or hungry, whether living in plenty or in want" (v. 12 NIV).

I knew Christianity claims to offer peace and contentment in the midst of life's chaos and crazy, but as I read these words, I realized I had forgotten or had perhaps never known what that deep peace felt like. I had believed that peace was for someone like Paul but not for me.

Yet here was Paul, amid his own suffering, declaring to his friends in Philippi—and to me and you—that peace was not only possible but the result of deep faith. What did Paul know about trusting God that I did not? Did he possess a superhuman sense of peace that we non-apostles aren't capable of? Or did his miraculous conversion and incessant suffering lead him to sing—and to teach us to sing—of the contentment available to all of us? My exploration of Philippians sent me on a quest to find my missing peace.

Trusting the Truth

We are first introduced to Paul in the book of Acts, where we find him persecuting Christians. He oversaw the murder of Stephen, a devout man who preached the gospel and served the poor (8:1). In Acts 9, we hear that Paul was "still breathing out murderous threats against the Lord's disciples" (v. 1 NIV).

But on his way to Damascus to abuse more Christians, Jesus met him. A blinding light sent him to the ground, and a voice spoke: "Saul, Saul, why are you persecuting me?" (v. 4). Paul asked who this was, and he was answered: "I am Jesus, the one you are persecuting" (v. 5).

In that moment, everything changed for Paul. Not because he had a random spiritual experience, but because he had discovered that what Christians believed about Jesus was actually true. Jesus was the resurrected Son of God—the hope of those Paul had been persecuting was real after all.

From that point on, Paul preached boldly, endured suffering, risked his life, and experienced peace and contentment because he banked his life on the truth that Jesus is the Messiah and author of salvation. In fact, Jesus Himself is the ultimate truth—in John 14:6, He said, "I am the way, the truth, and the life." Not the truth just for Paul, but the truth that can set everyone free.

Before Paul sang to the Philippians about rejoicing and finding peace, he sang to them a first-century hymn about who Jesus is—the humble king and Son of God, whom everyone from everywhere will bow before in worship one day. He insisted that his church friends sing this truth until it became their reality (Phil. 2:5–11).

One of the mantras of our culture is "Your deepest truth is found inside you, so you do you." In a certain sense, that's right. It's true that cheese makes me ill—so I'm going to avoid eating it, while others will embrace it as their favorite food. I love singing and songwriting but not math, so I'll go on tour instead of getting an accounting job.

But personal truth is not the type of truth Paul was talking about. Paul was talking about unchanging, universal truth—like the fact that murder is wrong or that kindness toward others is good. Paul based his life on the premise that Jesus is the unchanging truth for everyone.

Our feelings change often, so instead of living by "you do you," I base my life on a universal truth outside myself—a truth that remains constant, even when my feelings and circumstances change. The same truth that Paul based his life on.

Paul's Philippian friends needed to be reminded of this ultimate truth, just as we do. They were a motley crew of new believers: Lydia the fashionista, a shrewd businesswoman and devout Christian (Acts 16:14–15); the slave girl, a possessed fortune-teller who followed Paul around, shrieking that he was a man of God, until he healed her (vv. 16–18); and the prison guard who almost took his own life the night the chains fell off Paul and Silas but who changed course when he heard the truth of Christ (vv. 25–34).

With the truth of Jesus at the center, the young church was learning how to live in harmony despite their ethnic and class differences. There was no sense of "you do you"; they didn't live by what felt right to them, regardless of who it affected. They were, however, beginning to experience persecution because of their faith. Paul based all his encouragement to sing in the darkness on the premise that the gospel of Christ was the reality on which they built their lives (Phil. 2:1–5).

If Jesus is truly the risen Son of God, it changes everything. Many consider Him to have been a devout moral teacher with exceptional character. But as C. S. Lewis said, "A man who was merely a man and said the sort of things Jesus said would not be a great moral teacher. He would either be a lunatic—on a level with the man who says he is a poached egg—or else he would be the Devil of Hell. You must make your choice. Either this man was, and is, the Son of God: or else a madman or something worse."[1]

If Christ is who He said He is, then He can absolutely be trusted with every worry and care we have. If the claims of Jesus are true, we are never fighting our battles alone, we aren't facing circumstances that are beyond His control, and we are being carried by someone who has experienced suffering and will one day demolish every bit of it.

In Matthew 11:28–29, Jesus said, "Come to me, all who labor and are heavy laden, and I will give you rest. Take my yoke upon you, and learn from me, for I am gentle and lowly in heart, and you will find rest for your souls" (ESV).

Life can often feel like a grind—especially as a believer. Loving our enemies (or even our neighbors and family) takes showing up and putting in the work. It isn't easy to be purposeful about doing what is good and right, especially when no one would notice if we made a different choice.

But Jesus as the risen Lord means we have hope! Not only is He an example to follow, but He has also given His all for our infinite joy and freedom. And He has sent the Spirit to empower us with all we need to love and live well.

Some days this truth may be all we have to hold on to, but it is truth worth basing our lives on!

Singing the Truth Together

I often get to experience seeing through the eyes of others. One of my favorite memories of this was after a show in Washington State. On a walk in the desert with my friends Kyle and Andrew, who played guitar and percussion with me, they both commented on how particularly beautiful the sky looked. Kyle explained to me that the sun was visible on one side of the sky and the moon on the other.

I tried to comprehend this but got nowhere. I'd always assumed that when the moon or sun could be seen, it filled the sky—or at least most of it. The guys were surprised at my theory and explained that, from our vantage point, the moon is never larger than their thumbnails. I was stunned. How could a thumbnail-sized object in the sky radiate enough light to be noticed by any eye?

Andrew further complicated matters in my mind's eye by explaining that he could see craters on the moon's surface. They looked like raised dots, he said. Fascinating! I soon discovered that stars appear as tiny dots of light in the sky. Until that moment, I'd always assumed they were the shape and size of the stars I've decorated my Christmas trees with. Clouds, in my mind, were thick and dark or light and wispy mounds of floating cotton balls. Now I was discovering they're much larger—more like small houses or even bigger.

I was equal parts deflated and fascinated, and I peppered them with questions for weeks afterward. I had to figure out what else in nature I'd imagined as different from the reality. It turned out that I needed the eyes of others to help me gain true perspective on the world.

Paul knew we all need that. We can't have a balanced viewpoint if we're listening only to ourselves. But he also knew it wouldn't be easy to trust one another and get along. He called the Philippians to "stand firm in the Lord" (4:1), knowing that Jesus will return and that the best is yet to come (3:20–21).

In chapter 4, he called two women leaders who were in disagreement to "agree in the Lord" (v. 2) and called for their fellow believers to help them do it (v. 3).[2] Paul wasn't saying, "Get along because God wants you to." He was saying, "Be humble and loving toward each other, even when you have differences, because that's what Christ would have done." As my friend Dr. Paul Jeon said, when we have the mind-set of Christ, "we can disagree without becoming disagreeable."[3]

Paul was also challenging the Philippians (and us) to spend ourselves in one another's lives as Jesus has invested in us. Because our names are written in the Book of Life, we know that there will come a day when our disagreements are dissolved for good.[4] Paul went on to call the church to "rejoice in the Lord always" and to be reasonable and gracious, because the Lord is near (vv. 4–5).

This is why the song of the church is set apart from that of all other faiths. But these are unbelievably challenging ideals for our very individualistic world. With political tensions and theological differences so intense, we will find peace only as we learn to do life together, even with our differences, and joyfully trust that God's Spirit is working in all of us. We cannot truly see God without each other's help, and we will not see and know how true and near He is until we invest in one another's lives.

One of the reasons my anxiety grew to a fever pitch was my lack of church community. My full travel schedule found me surrounded by people—but not people I was spiritually connected to. Friendships were often superficial or had a short shelf life, because companions would move or go out on different tours and we'd never connect again.

I told myself that even though this wasn't ideal, it was just a season. I was reading books about the spiritual life and listening to my fair share of sermons and podcasts, after all. Besides, I was with different church communities every day.

But not doing life day in and day out with the same folks meant I couldn't see God clearly. I wasn't being changed by the truth of the gospel. I didn't have anyone to call me out on unhealthy and unwise decisions. Because I had no deep church commitment and connection, I wasn't doing much rejoicing or learning to be gentle in a community. And as a result, I wasn't seeing the light of truth that could break through the dark of my anxiety and restlessness.

To make matters worse, when I was home, subtle lies about church began to creep in. When you sing sacred music and you happen to be blind, walking into church can be a bit of a harrowing experience. Either people know your music and awkwardly accost you to talk about it, or they don't know, and they awkwardly avoid you because you're blind. This became my banner excuse for getting to church just in time for the service and leaving right when it was over.

But Paul called us to get over ourselves and stop making excuses by showing us his own need for other people. He called the Philippians his "joy and crown," those he "loved and longed for" (4:1).

Even though Paul had personally met Jesus, was made an official apostle, and had a full schedule planting and growing churches, his Christian friendships brought him joy and encouragement he couldn't live without. He needed their love, their care, and their prayers.

I have come to see that my singing, writing, and thinking are all *off* when I don't have community. But when I do, things are different. Listening and being listened to, seeking and offering wisdom, asking for prayer, worshipping, and just doing life with believers I'm connected to—all these practices lead me to see tangible evidence of God's love and to sing more confidently of what is true.

Talking to God on our own is a key part of learning to sing in every situation, of course. But we all know that many negative things happen in our minds when we're alone with our fears and our phones. We get more anxious and more illogical. We get confused about what's true and what's important. It has been my experience that God speaks much louder to us through other people than He does when we're trying to navigate life alone.

That does not make it easy. Church can be one of the hardest spaces for many of us to find our place. It still is for me. But it will always be the most important place for us to find and reflect Christ.

The Way to Be Worry-Free

In Philippians 4:6–7, Paul told us to not be anxious about anything. Instead, he said, take your requests and your thankfulness to God, and peace that you can't even comprehend will surround you and protect your minds in Jesus.

Paul didn't suggest that we not be anxious—he commanded it. Which shows, at the very least, that it's possible to not be anxious. Why would he command us to do something that is impossible? Paul never said God would answer our worries according to our wishes. But he said, to paraphrase, "Don't worry; pray." Or as Martin Luther said, "Pray, and let God worry."[5]

Similarly, Peter ordered us to throw all our anxieties on God because He cares for us (1 Pet. 5:7).

The key here is that we bring those worries to Him with gratitude. In the Bible, we often hear of people full of fear about what was about to happen or devastated by what had happened, yet they recounted God's faithfulness as they prayed.

I have come to love recounting to God how He has been faithful, because it instantly changes my perspective. Sometimes I go back to Leah, Moses, and even Adam and Eve. It's mind-blowing that the God who spoke to them also listens to and speaks to us and cares about our lives.

Every night now, I make a gratitude list of at least five things I'm thankful for. No matter what kind of day I've had, I start writing as I pray, and I rarely end up with only five things on that list. By the time I get to my requests, I feel a renewed confidence and peace because, as I look back over my day and over the history of God's faithfulness, I see how He truly cares and is at work in my life and in the lives of those in my space. I have a sense that even if my circumstances don't change, He will guide me through, as He has always done.

We learn through Paul's words to the Philippians that prayer is the place where God's strength overpowers our weakness and His faithfulness overcomes our fear and restlessness. Without prayer, there is no singing in the dark. There's no joy. No rest from anxiety. But prayer with gratitude enfolds our hearts with peace.

In the midst of my most restless hour, as I began to practice what Paul commanded, things began to change. For a season I served part-time as a worship leader in a Nashville church that had a couple of campuses. Though it proved to be the most rigorous of my musical experiences so far, it was a beautiful time of growth and change.

When I wasn't on the road, I was at my home church, leading worship and learning to be in community. I learned to forge ahead during the awkward moments of getting to know new people. I learned to keep showing up for small group, no matter how uncomfortable or even outright boring it could feel. And through sharing the lives of others, day in and day out, I gained a sense of grounding, leading to a peace I hadn't experienced before.

I also began to pray differently. I talked to God about everything that was going on, with a renewed belief that He saw and cared and could bring change. As I look back over my journals from that season, I can witness the transformation from virtually one-sided blubbering in a place of anxiety and discontentment to an awareness of God's greatness, holiness, and constant faithfulness.

New community and a deeper attention to Scripture and prayer led to a bigger view of God and began the evolution of a new, more peaceful me. I started to learn how to fight my tendency to worry. Instead of being dominated by stressful circumstances, I began to train my mind to move in the opposite direction—toward the peace of Christ. And I was able to let go of anxiety meds.

Worry and restlessness are constant battles—battles that most of us will face until eternity. And for some of us, medication serves as a life-changing aid to living fully and balanced. (Praise God for brilliant scientists.) But wherever we find ourselves on this spectrum, God longs to give us life-altering, soul-resonating peace through Himself, His Word, prayer, and community with other believers.

We Are What We Sing

Before he wrapped up his letter, Paul gave us a final weapon for our arsenal against anxiety: thinking on the things that are true, noble, right, pure, lovely, admirable, excellent, and praiseworthy (4:8). As Dr. Jeon said, Paul told the Philippians to "pay attention to what they pay attention to."[6]

I relate everything to music, so I've come to think this way: we all have a theme song that's playing constantly on repeat in our minds. It's whatever song our circumstances have taught us to sing, and it usually isn't positive or peace filled. It wakes us up in the morning and plays in the background all day. When we are squeezed by life, it comes to the fore.

The truth is that this song will be stuck on repeat until we figure out how to sing something else.

Paul knew that. There are lots of theme songs he could have chosen to sing. His background music could have been a song of pride because he was well educated, devout, and moral. His theme song could have been one of shame for all the terrible things he had done to Christians before he met Jesus. He could have sung a song of bitterness because, as an apostle, he lived in a constant state of suffering.

Instead, Paul's theme song in chapter 4 is astoundingly beautiful: "Rejoice in the Lord." "Do not be anxious." "The peace of God, which transcends all understanding, will guard your hearts." "Whatever is true … think about such things." "I have learned the secret of being content in any and every situation." (vv. 4, 6, 7, 8, 12 NIV)

True Power

How can we, like Paul, choose a theme song about the power and beauty of Christ? The first thing we have to do is actually learn a new song. Then we can start to sing it.

Memorizing is the secret to everything I do in life. Because it's difficult to read braille and play piano at the same time, I memorize all my music, including the worship songs I lead on Sundays. I've also been memorizing Greek and Hebrew paradigms in seminary over the last couple of years.

I don't have total recall, so I memorize by singing. I've discovered that this is my current superpower. If I can sing a paradigm, I memorize it quickly and never forget it. Because of this, I often wake up with the new worship song I led last weekend or the Hebrew paradigm for suffixed pronouns playing in my mind.

I've finally figured out that I should memorize Scripture by singing it too. So every day, I sing some Scripture. A few days of this and I have it memorized. When I'm riddled with anxiety, I sing it. When I'm grumpy or discontented, I sing it again. It reminds me of the unchangeable truths I trust.

Maybe you've always liked the idea of memorizing what the Bible says but you've got it filed away as an interesting idea to consider someday when life slows down. But we are all memorizing every day. Movie lines. Song lyrics. The images and words we find on social media. The ideas our culture says are important, especially the negative things people say. I've read that our brains hold on most tightly to the things that have brought a negative emotional reaction.[7] It seems to me, then, that the only way to counteract all the negative noise trapped inside us is to take Paul's advice by memorizing what's lovely until that's the song on repeat in our brains.

I recently heard a story from some missionaries who serve in a country where witch doctors and sorcerers are prevalent. One day, two malnourished young brothers were brought to the orphanage the missionaries run, clinging to each other and petrified of everything. They had been rescued from a witch doctor's property and were clearly traumatized. The caregivers would go in at night to find the boys huddled together in the far corner under their bed, shaken from visions they had seen.

Fast-forward several years: the boys are strong, well adjusted, successful at school, and devout Christ followers. The key to this change? Memorizing verse upon verse of Scripture. As soon as the boys began learning the Word, they began praying it in every moment of fear, and it gave them peace. It took root in their lives and profoundly changed them. If the Word has the power to change those who have been to hell and back, doesn't it also hold power for you and me?

Paul made Christ's love the song on repeat in his mind. He promised the Philippians that if they followed suit, the God of peace would be with them (Phil. 4:9). What Paul was saying here is the thing that is riveting about the Christian faith: It is not a formula we follow but a person. It is God with us—and an invitation to hear His voice and to know and be with Him.

As we pray, as His truths become more beautiful to us, and as we reach for connection with others, we get a deeper sense of Him. His peace becomes louder than our worry. His rest replaces our discontentment. As we set our eyes on Him, we see that He is with us in every situation.

The Bigger Story: Don't Box Jesus In

One thing that has clicked for me since understanding Paul better is that I have often put Jesus in a box. I am thankful for salvation and knowing that the best days are yet to come. But what I often forget is that Christ died not only to save us when we die but also to bring us joy and contentment today. Here on this planet.

When we are brought from death to life, God implants the hope of heaven in us. That hope—of seeing Jesus face to face and of worshipping God endlessly—should pour out of our lives as believers now.[8] This hopeful, joyful inner peace is meant to free us from our time-wasting worry.

The result of Paul's song of contentment was a balanced perspective on his circumstances. No matter how bad things got, he was centered, joyfully and fearlessly pursuing the next thing. His trials were miniscule compared to the trial Christ had gone through for him. Paul remained content, despite what he had or didn't have, as he trusted what was true, surrounded himself with community that helped him stand in the truth, and sang songs of thankful praise.

We can do what Paul did: breathe in God's faithful promises and breathe out prayers of praise and thanksgiving, because we can face any suffering through Christ, who gives us strength (Phil. 4:13). When we follow Paul's practices, contentment and peace grow louder and a deep truth resonates: "The secret is *Christ* in *me*, not me in a different set of circumstances."[9]

I'm learning how different a day looks when the love of Christ is the loudest song—the one on repeat—in my mind. When it is, I'm more courageous in loving and pursuing people. I'm quicker to meet their needs instead of being wrapped up in my own. I'm more forgetful of the wrongs done to me, knowing I'm perfectly loved and understood by the One whose mind thought up all of us. And no matter what's going on outside of me, calm reverberates inside.

Your Song of Inner Peace

Consider where Paul's story intersects yours. Are you singing a song of peace and contentment? If not, do you want to be?

Write your song below. Perhaps you need to lay down the things that keep you from being content. Or you could ask God to help you truly believe that He is faithful and good, even when you can't see it. To help inspire you, here are some words from one of my favorite old hymns:

> *God moves in a mysterious way*
> *His wonders to perform;*
> *He plants His footsteps in the sea*
> *And rides upon the storm.*
>
> *Deep in unfathomable mines*
> *Of never-failing skill,*
> *He treasures up His bright designs*
> *And works His sov'reign will.*
>
> *Ye fearful saints, fresh courage take;*
> *The clouds you so much dread*
> *Are big with mercy and shall break*
> *In blessings on your head.*[10]

Hearing God's Song

Let's memorize and practice Paul's words of truth this week until calm reverberates in our minds: ***"Do not be anxious about anything, but in every situation, by prayer and petition, with thanksgiving, present your requests to God. And the peace of God, which transcends all understanding, will guard your hearts and your minds in Christ Jesus" (Phil. 4:6–7 NIV)***.

Let's also memorize Jesus' words of comfort to us: ***"Don't let your heart be troubled. Believe in God; believe also in me" (John 14:1)***.

Then I saw a new heaven and a new earth; for the first heaven and the first earth had passed away, and the sea was no more. I also saw the holy city, the new Jerusalem, coming down out of heaven from God, prepared like a bride adorned for her husband.

Then I heard a loud voice from the throne: Look, God's dwelling is with humanity, and he will live with them. They will be his peoples, and God himself will be with them and will be their God. He will wipe away every tear from their eyes. Death will be no more; grief, crying, and pain will be no more, because the previous things have passed away.

Then the one seated on the throne said, "Look, I am making everything new." He also said, "Write, because these words are faithful and true." Then he said to me, "It is done! I am the Alpha and the Omega, the beginning and the end. I will freely give to the thirsty from the spring of the water of life...."

He then carried me away in the Spirit to a great, high mountain and showed me the holy city, Jerusalem, coming down out of heaven from God, arrayed with God's glory....

I did not see a temple in it, because the Lord God the Almighty and the Lamb are its temple. The city does not need the sun or the moon to shine on it, because the glory of God illuminates it, and its lamp is the Lamb.

Revelation 21:1–6, 10–11, 22–23

Chapter 10

Singing in the Light

Our Dreams, God's Dreams

As a kid, I had endless dreams for the future. Among them, living and songwriting in LA, being crowned Miss America, and becoming a professional Girl Scout—whatever that is. By the time I got to high school, however, my dreams had shrunk significantly. I imagined staying close to home or skipping off to college after whichever boy I happened to have a crush on at the moment. Between my freshman and senior years, many of my songs reflected this focus on the moment rather than the bigger things of life.

When my youth pastor told me about Belmont University in Nashville and their spectacular music program, I thought it sounded interesting, but I had little expectation of ending up there. However, within a week of applying, I had a full scholarship and the prospect of a season of my life I could never have imagined. This was one small hint that God's big picture looked nothing like mine.

As I tried to find my way into Belmont's ensembles and pop music scene, I discovered there was no place for me. But as I talked about in an earlier chapter, I grew more excited by the prospect of a career as a high school choral director, and I poured myself into that work. Dead-end interviews led to a season of waiting—and then to an open door to write and share the music that I had thought would forever stay between me, my inner circle, and God. Again I heard the resounding truth that the Lord's plans looked nothing like mine.

A year or so into my music career, the world moved at breakneck speed every hour of the day, and I began to dream of doing something different. I declared to a friend that though this new life had some cool elements, I would be changing course soon. I definitely didn't want to do it for more than another year or so.

My fantasy at that point was to become a travel agent. I found the hunt for great deals on flights and hotels a rejuvenating part of my work, so I thought maybe I would take a step back from being onstage every night and book trips for other people's leisure, or perhaps to get them to *their* evenings onstage. Amid the noise of that hectic life, I was still trying to plan a path I could manage by myself—I was still dreaming small, my calling drowned out by the chaos of that season. But in His grace, the Lord did not give up on me. When I tried to give in to the things I could imagine, He moved me forward.

After finishing my record deal, after my mom's cancer, and after several years of teaching songwriting at Belmont and leading worship at a Nashville church while treading water with my own music, a close friend challenged me to consider what it exactly was that God had called me to. "Your plate is always full with things to do, Ginny," he said. "But have you stopped to pray and listen and allow God to speak to you about what direction He's leading you?"

As you've heard, by that point my various life seasons had led me to sing a deeper, richer song of hope. My friend's words led me to my next season. As I began to ask God to open my eyes to what work I should focus my energy on, my work life did a 180. The change was imperceptible at first, but with time came momentum. A couple of years later, I was back to full-time writing, singing, and speaking, and I would soon be pursuing seminary.

In this last chapter, I would like you to consider a question: How are you singing in the dark—in the haze of uncertainty or in the clouds of sadness and separation from God?

It seems to me there are really only a couple of choices for how to navigate this dark world. Without God, either we grumble and muddle our way through or we're intentional about trying to cultivate inner positivity or peace. Either way, we are solely responsible for creating our song.

When we know God, we still have a couple of choices. We can muddle through with a "sometimes song," asking God to help us when we're facing difficult times and occasionally singing in half-hearted praise when the mood strikes us. Or we can turn our hearts to Him and live in a state of singing His song. When we do so, our songs are not only praises for the good and beautiful but also lament for the dark, difficult, and unfair. But always in this song there is hope. Hope that we can, even now, find joy in sorrow. Hope that our brightest days are ahead. Hope that our "momentary light affliction is producing for us an absolutely incomparable eternal weight of glory" (2 Cor. 4:17).

Thinking Big

These days, I love writing and singing more than I ever have, because I am no longer at the center of the work. Pursuing creative work is not for the faint of heart, but I am content and confident that it is the right path for me, at least in this season. The biggest change has been that my hope and worth are no longer wrapped up in my calling but in the One who has given it to me.

Though there would have been nothing wrong with staying near home, becoming a travel agent, or teaching, my dreams were always what was within reach. They were what *I* could imagine. But in His grace, God gave me a heart for the things He wanted me to do and the strength to do them.

All of us are called to live connected to God's plans—not only the ones for this life but also the plans for beyond this life, the plans that are truly beyond our comprehension. We tend to dream small. As C. S. Lewis so eloquently stated,

> It would seem that Our Lord finds our desires not too strong, but too weak. We are half-hearted creatures, fooling about with drink and sex and ambition when infinite joy is offered us, like an ignorant child who wants to go on making mud pies in a slum because he cannot imagine what is meant by the offer of a holiday at the sea. We are far too easily pleased.[1]

We've spent a lot of time talking about how to sing in the darkness of this life, how God empowers our songs with His hope for each day we're alive. But in this last chapter, we must discuss the most important part of our song—the hook.

The hook is the melodic and lyrical focal point of a song, the part you repeat again and again. If the hook is written well, you won't be able to get it out of your head. You'll never forget it.

The hook of our song in the dark is simply "the best is yet to come."

But how can we sing about what we can barely imagine? How can we yearn for eternity when our dreams for this life are too small? How can we ache for forever when we are far too easily pleased in the here and now?

I'm more convinced than ever that living out our calling to the glory of God gives our lives the deepest delight. But meditating on and singing about what's ahead is the core of our song of hope. God wants our minds fixed on Him and what it will be like to be with Him all day, every day.

Destined for a Greater Glory

I've had a lot of really fabulous life experiences—things I never thought I'd do as I sat at the out-of-tune reddish-oak upright piano all those years ago. I'm now friends with some of the folks whose music inspired me growing up. I've even met a couple of presidents, gotten a few number-one songs, won a few awards, and connected with people all over the world.

I haven't had much time to consider the magnitude of those adventures until recent years. Instead, like most self-employed songwriters, I've spent every day asking, "How can we build on this thing? How can we get it right?" With every new music release comes months of planning—choosing marketing strategies and creating images. I've lived my adult life plotting the next move and pivoting again and again.

These days, however, what I mostly ask myself is, *Am I useful yet? Does my life sing to others of the light that is to come?*

I don't think this way because I've reached some pinnacle of spirituality. Far from it. But life has taught me that my plans are always too simple. My dreams are too small, always based on what I can do, not on what God can do. Not only that, but nothing I manage to accomplish on this planet will ever be enough to satisfy me or those who might be watching. Pursuing glory here is a silly waste of time. What's important today is to love and serve in anticipation of that coming glory.

The glory of Christ, the glory to which we are being transformed, will be fully realized in eternity. There will be no need to plan, project an image, and pivot then. Instead, our new, glorious selves will do meaningful work, find great delight in caring for one another, and sing with full hearts to the God of all, the One who has given us Himself.

In Revelation 21, we get a taste of that coming glory. John showed us that our next life won't be lived in some ethereal land where we sit around on pillowy clouds, singing all day long with choirs of angels. We will sing, of course, but the picture is of infinitely more. Let's consider the hope that comprises the hook of our song in the dark.

The tenderhearted apostle John sang his unshakable song of the coming glory in his final years of life, in exile on an island. John knew something of earthly glory, at least among the members of the early church. When he was young, he spent his days as one of Jesus' twelve disciples. He had affectionately leaned against Him at the Last Supper and witnessed both His crucifixion and the awesome miracle of His resurrection. Empowered by the Holy Spirit, John— along with Peter, Paul, and the other apostles—had performed signs and wonders and had spent his life shepherding the early church.

In Revelation, his final work, John wrote to seven churches, encouraging them in their faith and sharing all that God had shown him about the glory yet to come. As some of them faced seemingly endless persecution, he reminded them that this world was not their home. He exhorted them to hold on. Chapter 21 offers us a glimpse of the glory, beauty, and wonder that is promised to those who believe.

As we live in the "already" and the "not yet" tension of the Christian life, it's hard for us to imagine what this will be like. But when it comes to the age of forever, John gave us several concrete truths we can hold on to with hope.

The New City and the New Choir

John saw the new Jerusalem, "prepared like a bride," coming down from the new heaven to the new earth (Rev. 21:1–2). The new Jerusalem is the unified church in its "perfected and eternal state."[2] It is the bride of Christ. It is all the saints from all the ages coming together.

The prophet Isaiah began singing of this glorious time back when Israel was being exiled: "The redeemed of the LORD will return and come to Zion with singing, crowned with unending joy. Joy and gladness will overtake them, and sorrow and sighing will flee" (35:10 HCSB).

All those years later, Isaiah's song was taken up by John. And just like in Isaiah's day, John sang in the midst of much darkness. Isaiah had laid out for God's people the darkness of uncertainty, fear, and suffering they would face in their years of exile. John was writing to churches who lived amid the darkness of persecution and powerlessness in their own society. The song in the hearts of the

Israelites and the young church was largely the same: "Where is the Lord? When will He come to rescue us?" Both John and Isaiah sang to the people of the day of infinite hope—the day when we, all the saints from all the ages, will sing together in light.

The group of believing saints, as diverse and messy as they are, will become one united, beautiful, overjoyed bride who cannot keep from singing. How can we imagine this?

For one thing, that person who always ends up in the row behind you on Sundays, singing off-key during worship and bending your ear with all the stories of her woes before you can scuttle out after the service, will be standing next to you, bellowing a beautiful melody that fits perfectly with your harmony. And you'll absolutely love singing with her!

Surrounding you will be people from everywhere. As Shai Linne said, "The Lord Jesus Christ is so glorious that one people group is not enough to reflect his greatness. He wants all of them."[3]

John wrote earlier in this letter, "I looked, and there was a vast multitude from every nation, tribe, people, and language, which no one could number, standing before the throne and before the Lamb.... And they cried out in a loud voice: Salvation belongs to our God, who is seated on the throne, and to the Lamb!" (Rev. 7:9–10).

One of my favorite parts of living on this planet is the diversity of people. I first began to learn the beauty of the sound of our different voices and hearts at my predominantly African American school growing up. As I've traveled the world, my admiration for all the peoples God has made has grown immeasurably.

As I write this chapter, we are six months into the COVID-19 pandemic. My church here in the city gathers every morning for a time of prayer online. We're a pretty diverse crew, but our cries to the Lord for healing and change are lifted as one.

Heaven will be like this, except the song will not be one of lament, pleading, or anguish. It will be a song of joy, awe, and celebration. It will be sung to the Lord and the Lamb, who will be right there in our midst. Not some mysterious heavenly choir, but your voice and mine, your life experience and mine, raised together in the most perfect song of praise.

I think of how many people I've sung with here on earth whom I can't wait to sing with again. Like my dear cousin Christi, who passed away of brain cancer. I have a recording of us singing together when I was eight and she was eleven: "Oh Lord, our Lord, how majestic is your name in all the earth!" (Ps. 8:1).

We will sing again with Christi.

I remember playing and singing hymns with my grandpa, a kind and humble pastor with a big, booming preaching and singing voice. He sat beside me at the old upright, my eight-year-old fingers navigating the few keys in which I could play hymns. His bellowing voice sometimes cracked as he gamely reached for notes that were just beyond his reach, for the sole sake of singing with his granddaughter. I remember singing hymns of hopeful mourning without him as we laid him to rest after years of poor health.

We will sing again with Grandpa.

I recall singing with my friend Ronell, who was just twenty when she passed away:

> *When you know you're holding tighter to His hand,*
> *That's when you can say amen.*[4]

In her last days, she said to me, "Tomorrow I might wake up and find a miracle has happened to my body. Or tomorrow I might wake up in the arms of Jesus. Either way, I win."

When we have won, once and for all, we will join Ronell in song.

As you fill in the song with memories of the saints you've loved and lost, think also of the ones who have lived in ages past, whose songs of suffering and joy have stirred our hearts. Consider the saints whose stories have leapt off the pages of our Bibles. People like Leah, alone and unloved, except by her heavenly Father. Like Moses, the aged shepherd, whose heart came to look like God's. Like Hannah, who gave up her victimhood for a lifetime of joy and sacrifice. And the list goes on.

All the singers of God's hope from all over the world and all the ages will stand together, no longer lone voices in their suffering but united in their joy. United also by their stories of how the Lord brought them to this place, declaring that, indeed, nothing had separated them from the love of Christ (Rom. 8:39). They lived blocks or oceans apart. And months or centuries apart. But those who have known the joy of singing about God's hope in darkness will sing to Him together in perfect light.

Best of all, the One who sang hope to us down through the ages will be in our midst. We will sing to Him, and He will, as He has always done, sing over us.

As I reflect on this part of John's song, I'm guided to live wholeheartedly in community now. My inclination is always to reserve gobs of "me time," because it's easier than engaging with people who are messy (like me). But I realize that the beauty of life is found in our connection around the table now—a connection that is practice for when we are, one day, gathered as one around the throne.

Singing with the Lord and the Lamb

I love nothing more than a powerful voice that hits every note confidently, leading me to believe every word being sung. What will it be like when that voice is the Lord's?

In John's vision, the voice from heaven said, "Look, God's dwelling is with humanity, and he will live with them. They will be his peoples, and God himself will be with them and will be their God" (Rev. 21:3).

In ancient times, God's people worshipped Him in His temple. It was the place where His glory lived. When Christ came, He became the temple, in the flesh, walking among His people. We now have the Holy Spirit living and working in our hearts, the new temple where Jesus dwells. We're being made ready for the day when the Lord and the Lamb will again be physically present with us. Forever. With no more separation.

"The city does not need the sun or the moon to shine on it, because the glory of God illuminates it, and its lamp is the Lamb" (v. 23). On that day, we will be face to face with the God to whom we've cried out, expressing our longings, our questions, our laments. No longer will we speak our prayers into the silence, wishing for an audible answer. We will forever be in the presence of the Father, who has brought us to Himself, and the Son, who has given Himself for the joy of making that possible (Heb. 12:2). The Light will sing with us and over us.

We, the bride, will have the best wedding day imaginable, the first wedding for many of us. We will marry the One we were made for, the One whose image we bear. The One who surpasses all glory. We will love Him more than anything we've ever loved.

There will be an endless amount to discover and uncover about Him. We'll never get bored. Think about your most favorite person now, the one whose fascinating stories and interesting sides have no end. In the new heaven and the new earth, that person will be the Lord, and we will be endlessly discovering who He is.

The Bigger Story

Paul told the Corinthians and us that if we are in Christ, we are now a new creation. He called us to live in that newness (2 Cor. 5:17). As we "put on the new self, the one created according to God's likeness" (Eph. 4:24), we are being transformed into that likeness by the Spirit (2 Cor. 3:18).

Though our bodies and minds are wasting away as we go, our hearts are being renovated, learning to love the things God loves. We press on toward that goal of living in our newness in spirit and action. But what will it look like when our bodies, hearts, and minds are completely renewed once and for all?

I often think about what I can't see. The crystal blue of the ocean. The majesty of the mountains. The smile of a friend. And yet, I know I'm not alone in my blindness. The apostle Paul said that, for all of us, the glass is blurry just now. We're all blind in a certain sense. Blinded by our guilt, our pain, and by the fact that we are human, unable to see the future or the heavenly realms. But Paul said there will be a brilliant day when you and I finally see! We will gaze on Jesus' face, fully captivated by His beauty, "even as [we are] fully known" (1 Cor. 13:12 NIV).

In this final newness, my blindness and yours will be gone. In an instant we will understand that all our sufferings always had infinite purpose. Our new, perfectly loving hearts will replace our misguided ones. My need to people-please and perform will never plague me again. Neither will your sins and struggles plague you. Many of our deepest longings will fade away, and some will be fulfilled in greater ways than we could ever have imagined.

When the Alpha and Omega makes everything new, death, grief, and pain will be no more. On that day, He whose hands formed and renewed creation will wipe every tear from your eyes and mine once and for all (Rev. 21:4–5). As we embrace that newness in our resurrected, perfectly working bodies—with hearts that love the good and beautiful and hands that are eager to do great work—we will hear the echoes of Jesus' words on the cross in our Father's final pronouncement: "It is finished!" (Rev. 21:6 NLT; John 19:30).

In the words of renowned speaker Joni Eareckson Tada, "The best we can hope for in this life is a knothole peek at the shining realities ahead. Yet a glimpse is enough. It's enough to convince our hearts that whatever sufferings and sorrows currently assail us aren't worthy of comparison to that which waits over the horizon."[5]

As we fix our minds on the hook of our song in the dark, "the best is yet to come," we can sing enthusiastically with the apostle John, "Come, Lord Jesus!" (Rev. 22:20).

Your Song of Hope

During the early days of the coronavirus pandemic, at seven o'clock each night in New York City, many people would go out onto their fire escapes or stick their heads out their windows to cheer for the frontline workers. Some folks would get in their cars and honk their horns. Others brought out their trumpets and saxophones and blew a few celebratory notes. Some banged on pots and pans. And some guy always brought his boom box to blare a song of enthusiasm, which everyone clapped and sang along to. It was the most joyful moment of the day.

There is something about all sorts of folks who don't know each other cheering for the same thing that makes your heart hopeful. But if this evening rally was a sweet, hopeful moment, imagine what it will be like when you and I—and all the rest of God's people— sing together with Him in our midst! I cannot wait to sing with you! And I pray that as we've journeyed through these songs together and as you've heard the voices of these biblical singers and seen how God worked in their lives, your voice has grown stronger.

In our final songwriting venture, I want you to write your hope for the future. Think about what you're looking forward to being healed of and who you can't wait to see again. Imagine what it will be like to see Jesus face to face. To gaze on Him or to fall at His feet. To know even as we are fully known. Here are some words to get you started:

> *There is a king, who left a kingdom,*
> *Sent to die and rise again, our lives to save.*
> *There'll come a day when our eyes behold Him,*
> *And we will gaze upon the fullness of His grace.*
> *Our taste of heaven has just begun.*
> *Great is this love, with greater still to come.*[6]

Singing God's Song

As we think about what it will mean to never sing in the dark again, let's memorize and meditate on these words: *"He will wipe away every tear from their eyes. Death will be no more; grief, crying, and pain will be no more, because the previous things have passed away" (Rev. 21:4).*

And finally, let's sing the Lord's song: *"He said to me, 'It is done! I am the Alpha and the Omega, the beginning and the end. I will freely give to the thirsty from the spring of the water of life'" (Rev. 21:6).*

I pray that as you've brought before Him your own songs, laments, and prayers, you've been changed—by His greatness and power and tender love for you. I pray that you and I will keep exploring the songs of Scripture, memorizing them and letting them lead us into worship and move us to sing—in any darkness we face.

Acknowledgments

As I embarked on writing *Singing in the Dark*, I quickly discovered that authoring chapters in a book is nothing like crafting lyrics for a three-minute song. I have learned much through the process and am so appreciative of those who have patiently guided me on my journey.

My deepest gratitude is to my faithful, long-suffering editor and friend, Rachel Lulich. Thank you for your hours of answering my questions about best practices for book-writing, offering opinions, and, of course, editing and helping me edit multiple rounds of this manuscript. I have no idea how I would have made it to the finish line without your patience and valuable insight. Thank you a thousand times over!

To Joni Eareckson Tada, Christy Nockels, Michael Card, Nancy Guthrie, Kelly Minter, Lisa Harper, Susie Larson, Jeremy Camp, and Michael W. Smith: Thank you so much for your generous written words of support and endorsement. Each of you has meaningfully marked my life with your testimony of God's goodness and truth.

To those who have generously granted me permission to share parts of their stories in this book—Mom, Emily, John, Octavia, Aunt Carol, Jeremy and the Rescue:Freedom crew, Kori, and Charlynn—I am truly grateful. Your stories have made my story much richer.

To Hillary Manton Lodge: Thank you for your valuable insight as an author, and for generously giving your time to help me think through titles and big ideas.

I am also so grateful to the team at David C Cook, who took a manuscript and turned it into a book. Each of you has been marvelous to work with, and I so appreciate your hard work and dedication!

To Susan McPherson: Thank you for graciously championing this project (and me) from our first conversation. Your kindness and encouragement have made this process a delightful experience.

To Stephanie Bennett, who spearheaded my DCC team: I have so appreciated your joyful positivity along the way.

To Jeff Gerke, who patiently and generously provided content editing for the manuscript: I am so thankful for your insights and to have had the opportunity to work with you.

To Kayla Fenstermaker: Thank you for your diligence and for providing brilliant copyediting.

To Judy Gillispie: Thank you for being a delightful light throughout this book-creating process.

I also must thank the many individuals who have supported me, not only with this book, but in life.

To Andy Osenga: I so appreciate your friendship, your encouragement, and your effort to connect all the dots to bring this project to fruition.

To David McCollum: Thank you so much for blessing me with your kind and generous spirit, your patience, your loyalty, and your endless talents as manager, designer, sometimes-photographer, and the rest too numerous to mention here. I am grateful beyond words.

To Grace Kornegay: Thank you so much for everything you do to help my world run smoothly. I so appreciate your patience and generous spirit.

To Tyrus Morgan: You, Casey, and the kids are such a magnificent blessing in my life! Thank you for being a wonderful cowriter, producer, and friend, and for graciously allowing me to share some of our lyrics in the pages of this book.

To my seminary professors and cohort: What an unbelievable gift it has been to study with and learn from each of you! My experience of Christ has been deepened and enriched by your teaching, insights, and encouragement.

To Bob Lackey and the Imagine One Team: Thank you for blessing me with your friendship, encouragement, and support! It is a true privilege to know you!

To my fabulous family: I love you all and am so appreciative of your prayers, encouragement, support, and of how you taught me to love Scripture.

To my beautiful friends: Thank you for speaking truth to me and loving me well. I am truly blessed by each and every one of you in more ways than you know!

To the Lord who gives us the strength, courage, and means to sing in every darkness, and the songs with which to do it. How dark, empty, and meaningless life would be without Your perfect, radiant, life-altering light!

Notes

Introduction

1. Frances J. Crosby, "Blessed Assurance," 1873, public domain.

Chapter 1: A Song of Undivided Praise

1. For further insights on the story of Leah, see Derek Kidner, *Genesis*, Tyndale Old Testament Commentaries (Downers Grove, IL: InterVarsity, 1967), 170–73, and Timothy J. Keller, "The Girl Nobody Wanted" (sermon, Redeemer Presbyterian Church, New York City, October 11, 1998).

2. Andrew Murray, *The Believer's Daily Renewal* (Bloomington, MN: Bethany House, 1981), 23.

3. Ginny Owens and Andrew Osenga, "You Alone," *Sing Hope in the Darkness*, Integrity Music, 2021.

Chapter 2: A Song for the Plodding Path

1. Daniel I. Block, *Deuteronomy*, The NIV Application Commentary (Grand Rapids, MI: Zondervan, 2012), 748.

2. Joni Eareckson Tada and Steve Estes, *A Step Further: Growing Closer to God through Hurt and Hardship* (Grand Rapids, MI: Zondervan, 2001), 137.

3. Eleanor Henrietta Hull and Mary Elizabeth Byrne, "Be Thou My Vision," 1927, public domain, arrangement by Ginny Owens and Tyrus Morgan, *Sing Hope in the Darkness*, Integrity Music, 2021.

Chapter 3: A Song of Victory

1. See D. A. Carson, *Praying with Paul: A Call for Spiritual Reformation*, 2nd ed. (Grand Rapids, MI: Baker Academic, 2014), 33–44.

2. K. Lawson Younger Jr., *Judges and Ruth*, The NIV Application Commentary (Grand Rapids, MI: Zondervan, 2002), 151–52.

3. Younger, *Judges and Ruth*, 153.

4. Younger, *Judges and Ruth*, 154.

5. Ginny Owens, *I Know a Secret,* ChickPower Music, 2014.

6. Ginny Owens and Tyrus Morgan, "Inheritance," *Sing Hope in the Darkness*, Intergrity Music, 2021.

Chapter 4: A Song of Strength

1. Paul S. Evans, *1–2 Samuel*, ed. Tremper Longman III and Scot McKnight, The Story of God Bible Commentary (Grand Rapids, MI: Zondervan, 2018), 39.

2. David Steindl-Rast, "How to Be Grateful in Every Moment (but Not for Everything)," interview by Krista Tippett, *On Being*, January 21, 2016, https://onbeing.org/programs/david-steindl-rast-how-to-be-grateful-in-every-moment.

3. Ginny Owens and Andrew Gullahorn, "Thank You," *Expressions II: Wonder*, ChickPower Music, 2021.

4. Timothy J. Keller, *The Freedom of Self-Forgetfulness* (Chorley, UK: 10Publishing, 2012), 32.

5. Ginny Owens, "Made for More," *I Know a Secret*, ChickPower Music, 2014.

Chapter 5: A Song of Rest

1. Ryan Holiday, "How to Use Stoicism to Choose Alive Time over Dead Time," episode 419, April 9, 2020, *The Tim Ferriss Show*, www.youtube.com/watch?v=7Iknv6rt9uk.

2. Billy Graham, foreword to *Unto the Hills: A Daily Devotional* (Nashville, TN: Thomas Nelson, 2010).

3. Derek Kidner, *Psalms 1–72*, Kidner Classic Commentaries (Downers Grove, IL: InterVarsity, 2008), 127.

4. Timothy Keller and Kathy Keller, *The Songs of Jesus: A Year of Daily Devotions in the Psalms* (New York: Viking, 2015), February 10.

5. Tremper Longman III, *Psalms: An Introduction and Commentary*, Tyndale Old Testament Commentaries (Downers Grove, IL: InterVarsity, 2014), 137.

6. Katharina A. von Schlegel, "Be Still, My Soul," trans. Jane L. Borthwick, 1855, public domain, arrangement by Ginny Owens, *Say Amen: Hymns and Songs of Faith*, 2009.

Chapter 6: A Lament for the Misoriented Life

1. Derek Kidner, *Psalms 1–72*, Kidner Classic Commentaries (Downers Grove, IL: InterVarsity, 2008), 206.

2. Kidner, *Psalms 1–72*, 209.

3. Drawn from Barbara Miller Juliani in C. John Miller, *Saving Grace: Daily Devotions from Jack Miller* (Greensboro, NC: New Growth Press, 2014), xv.

4. Horatio G. Spafford, "It Is Well with My Soul," 1873, public domain.

Chapter 7: God's Song of Justice and Mercy

1. Robert B. Chisholm Jr., *Handbook on the Prophets* (Grand Rapids, MI: Baker Academic, 2002), 128.

2. Michael J. Wilkins, *Matthew*, The NIV Application Commentary (Grand Rapids, MI: Zondervan, 2004), 821.

3. Justo L. González, *The Story of Christianity*, vol. 1, *The Early Church to the Dawn of the Reformation* (New York: HarperOne, 2010), 114; Catherine Kroeger, "The Neglected History of Women in the Early Church," *Christianity Today*, 1988, www.christianitytoday.com/history/issues/issue-17/neglected-history-of -women-in-early-church.html.

4. Julian, "To Arsacius, High-Priest of Galatia," in *The Works of the Emperor Julian*, trans. Wilmer Cave Wright (London: William Heineman, 1923), 3:71.

5. Frances Ridley Havergal, "Take My Life," 1874, public domain.

Chapter 8: A Lament for the Broken World

1. "Christi Griggs Dippel: Sherwood, AR, 1972–2014," *Arkansas Democrat-Gazette*, April 30, 2014, www.arkansasonline.com/obituaries/2014/apr/30/christi -dippel-2014-04-30.

2. Samuel Trevor Francis, "O the Deep, Deep Love of Jesus," 1875, public domain. Ginny and Christi's version is found on *I Know a Secret*, ChickPower Music, 2014.

3. Josh Larsen, *Movies Are Prayers: How Films Voice Our Deepest Longings* (Downers Grove, IL: InterVarsity, 2017), 51.

4. Timothy Keller, *The Grieving Sisters*, The Encounters with Jesus Series (New York: Dutton, 2013).

5. Tremper Longman III, *Psalms: An Introduction and Commentary*, Tyndale Old Testament Commentaries (Downers Grove, IL: InterVarsity, 2014), 132.

6. Derek Kidner, *Psalms 1–72*, Kidner Classic Commentaries (Downers Grove, IL: InterVarsity, 2008), 124–25.

7. Longman, *Psalms*, 133.

8. Mark Vroegop, *Dark Clouds, Deep Mercy: Discovering the Grace of Lament* (Wheaton, IL: Crossway, 2019), 191.

9. D. A. Carson, *Praying with Paul: A Call to Spiritual Reformation*, 2nd ed. (Grand Rapids, MI: Baker Academic, 2014), 155–56.

10. Kidner, *Psalms 1–72*, 126.

11. Ginny Owens, Tyrus Morgan, and Leslie Jordan, "Sing in the Darkness," *Sing Hope in the Darkness*, Integrity Music, 2021.

Chapter 9: A Song of Inner Peace

1. C. S. Lewis, *Mere Christianity* (New York: HarperOne, 2001), 52.

2. R. T. France, *New Bible Commentary*, Matthew 24:1–25:46 (Downers Grove, IL: IVP Academic, 1994), 935–937.

3. Paul S. Jeon, *Empowered by Joy: Reflections on Paul's Letter to the Philippians* (Eugene, OR: Wipf & Stock, 2012), 81.

4. Jeon, *Empowered by Joy*, 81.

5. Martin Luther, letter of February 10, 1546, in Eric W. Gritsch, *The Wit of Martin Luther* (Minneapolis: Augsburg Fortress, 2006), 64.

6. Jeon, *Empowered by Joy*, 86.

7. Allie Caren, "Why We Often Remember the Bad Better than the Good," *Washington Post*, November 1, 2018, www.washingtonpost.com/science/2018 /11/01/why-we-often-remember-bad-better-than-good.

8. The ideas of the previous two sentences are from Kyle Strobel, *Formed for the Glory of God: Learning from the Spiritual Practices of Jonathan Edwards* (Downers Grove, IL: InterVarsity, 2013), 21.

9. Elisabeth Elliot, *Keep a Quiet Heart* (Ann Arbor, MI: Vine Books, 1995), 20.

10. William Cowper, "God Moves in a Mysterious Way," 1774, public domain.

Chapter 10: Singing in the Light

1. C. S. Lewis, "The Weight of Glory," in *The Weight of Glory and Other Addresses* (New York: HarperOne: 2001), 26.

2. Robert H. Mounce, *The Book of Revelation*, rev. ed., The New International Commentary on the New Testament (Grand Rapids, MI: Eerdmans, 1998), 382.

3. Shai Linne, "Shai Linne on the Gospel and Ethnic Unity," *The Gospel Coalition Podcast*, April 17, 2020, www.thegospelcoalition.org/podcasts/tgc -podcast/ethnic-unity.

4. Ginny Owens and Ronell Ragbir, "Say Amen," *Say Amen: Hymns and Songs of Faith*, ChickPower Music, 2009.

5. Joni Eareckson Tada, *Glorious Intruder: God's Presence in Life's Chaos* (Colorado Springs, CO: Multnomah Books, 1989), 23.

6. Ginny Owens, Tyrus Morgan, and Leslie Jordan, "Greater Still to Come," *Sing Hope in the Darkness*, Integrity Music, 2021.

Sing Hope in the Darkness is a five-song set of hymns and worship anthems written for the church. These lyrics and melodies express rich, beautiful truths of the Christian faith and remind our hearts of the infinite ways God is good, true, and faithful to us. You will find excerpts from these songs throughout this book. May they serve as a guide and companion as we encourage one another to lift our voices and sing hope into the darkness!

With love,

Sing Hope in the Darkness Tracks

Inheritance

Greater Still to Come

Sing in the Darkness

Be Thou My Vision

You Alone

Available at all online music-streaming retailers